Kubernetes: Build and Deploy Modern Applications in a Scalable Infrastructure. The Complete Guide to the Most Modern Scalable Software Infrastructure.

Docker & Kubernetes, Volume 2

Jordan Lioy

Published by Jordan Lioy, 2023.

While every precaution has been taken in the preparation of this book, the publisher assumes no responsibility for errors or omissions, or for damages resulting from the use of the information contained herein.

KUBERNETES: BUILD AND DEPLOY MODERN APPLICATIONS IN A SCALABLE INFRASTRUCTURE. THE COMPLETE GUIDE TO THE MOST MODERN SCALABLE SOFTWARE INFRASTRUCTURE.

First edition. March 14, 2023.

ISBN: 979-8215530993

Written by Jordan Lioy.

Also by Jordan Lioy

Docker & Kubernetes

Docker: The Complete Guide to the Most Widely Used Virtualization Technology. Create Containers and Deploy them to Production Safely and Securely.
Kubernetes: Build and Deploy Modern Applications in a Scalable Infrastructure. The Complete Guide to the Most Modern Scalable Software Infrastructure.

Standalone

Software Containers: The Complete Guide to Virtualization Technology. Create, Use and Deploy Scalable Software with Docker and Kubernetes. Includes Docker and Kubernetes.

Table of Contents

Introduction to Kubernetes

In this book, we will assist you with learning to assemble and manage Kubernetes bunches. You will be given a portion of the basic container ideas and the operational setting, at every possible opportunity. All through the book, you'll be given examples that you can apply as you progress through the book. Before the finish of the book, you ought to have a strong foundation and even dabble in a portion of the more advance points, for example, federation and security.

This chapter will give a brief overview of containers and how they fill in as well as why management and orchestration are important to your business and/or venture team. The chapter will also give a brief overview of how Kubernetes orchestration can enhance our container management strategy and how we can get a basic Kubernetes group up, running, and ready for container deployments.

This chapter will incorporate the accompanying points:

- Presenting container operations and management

- Why container management is important?

- The advantages of Kubernetes

- Downloading the latest Kubernetes

- Installing and starting up another Kubernetes bunch

- The segments of a Kubernetes bunch

- A brief overview of containers

In recent years, containers have developed in popularity out of control. You would be hard-squeezed to attend an IT gathering without finding popular sessions on Docker or containers in general.

Docker lies at the heart of the mass adoption and the energy in the container space. As Malcom McLean upset the physical transportation world during the 1950s by creating a standardized dispatching container, which is utilized today for everything from ice shape trays to automobiles (you can allude to more details about this in point 1 in the References area at the finish of the chapter), Linux containers are changing the software advancement world by making application conditions portable and steady across the infrastructure landscape. As an organization, Docker has taken the current container innovation to another level by making it easy to execute and replicate across situations and suppliers.

What is a container?

At the center of the container, innovations are control gatherings (cgroups) and namespaces. Additionally, Docker utilizes association filesystems for added advantages to the container improvement process.

Cgroups work by allowing the host to share and also limit the assets each procedure or container can devour. This is important for both, asset utilization and security, as it counteracts denial-of-administration attacks on the host's hardware assets. Several containers can share CPU and memory while staying inside the predefined constraints.

Namespaces offer another type of isolation for process interaction inside operating frameworks. Namespaces limit the perceivability a procedure has on other procedures, organizing, filesystems, and client ID parts. Container forms are constrained to see just what is in the same namespace. Procedures from containers or the host forms are not straightforwardly accessible from inside this container procedure. Additionally, Docker gives each container its very own systems administration stack that ensures the attachments and interfaces in a similar fashion.

Association filesystems are also a key advantage of utilizing Docker containers. Containers run from an image. Much like an image in the VM or Cloud world, it speaks to state at a particular point in time. Container images snapshot the filesystem, however will in general be a lot smaller than a VM. The container shares the host bit and generally runs an a lot smaller arrangement of procedures, so the filesystem and boot strap period will in general be a lot smaller. Despite the fact that those constraints are not carefully upheld. Second, the association filesystem allows for proficient storage, download, and execution of these images.

The easiest way to understand association filesystems is to consider them like a layer cake with each layer baked freely. The Linux bit is our base layer; then, we may add an OS, for example, Red Hat Linux or Ubuntu. Next, we may add an application, for example, Nginx or Apache. Each change creates another layer. Finally, as you make changes and new layers are added, you'll always have a top layer (think icing) that is a writable layer.

What makes this really effective is that Docker caches the layers the first occasion when we construct them. In this way, suppose that we have an image with Ubuntu and then add Apache and assemble the image. Next, we fabricate MySQL with Ubuntu as the base. The subsequent form will be a lot faster because the Ubuntu layer is already cached. Essentially, our chocolate and vanilla layers, from the previous Layered filesystem figure, are already baked. We just need to bake the pistachio (MySQL) layer, assemble, and add the good to beat all).

For what reason are containers so cool?

Containers all alone are not another innovation and have in fact been around for a long time. What really separates Docker is the tooling and ease of utilization they have brought to the network. Present day improvement practices advance the utilization of Continuous Integration and Continuous Deployment. These procedures, when done right, can have a profound impact on your software item quality.

The advantages of Continuous Integration/Continuous Deployment

ThoughtWorks characterizes Continuous Integration as an improvement practice that expects engineers to integrate code into a shared archive several times each day. By having a continuous procedure of building and sending code, organizations are able to ingrain quality control and testing as part of the everyday work cycle. The outcome is that updates and bug fixes happen a lot faster and the overall quality improves.

Nonetheless, there has always been a challenge in creating advancement conditions that match that of testing and generation. Often irregularities in these conditions make it hard to gain the full advantage of continuous conveyance.

Utilizing Docker, engineers are currently able to have really portable deployments. Containers that are conveyed on an engineer's laptop are easily sent on an in-house staging server. They are then easily transferred to the creation server running in the cloud. This is because Docker develops containers with fabricate documents that indicate parent layers. One advantage of this is that it turns out to be exceptionally easy to guarantee OS, package, and application variants are the same across improvement, staging, and creation situations.

Because all the conditions are packaged into the layer, the same host server can have different containers running a variety of OS or package renditions. Further, we can have various languages and frameworks on the same host server without the typical reliance clashes we would get in a virtual machine (VM) with a solitary operating framework.

Resource utilization

The well-characterized isolation and layer filesystem also make containers ideal for running frameworks with a small impression and domain-explicit purposes. A streamlined deployment and release process means we can send rapidly and often. As such, many companies have diminished their deployment time from weeks or months to days and hours now and again. This improvement life cycle loans itself incredibly well to small, targeted teams dealing with small lumps of a larger application.

Microservices and orchestration

As we break down an application into quite certain domains, we need a uniform way to communicate between all the various pieces and domains. Web administrations have filled this need for a considerable length of time, however the added isolation and granular center that containers bring have paved a way for microservices.

The definition for microservices can be somewhat shapeless, however a definition from Martin Fowler, a regarded author and speaker on software improvement, says this (you can allude to more details about this in point 2 in the References area at the finish of the chapter):

So, the microservice architectural style is an approach to building up a solitary application as a suite of small administrations, each running in its very own procedure and communicating with lightweight mechanisms, often an HTTP resource API. These administrations are worked around business capabilities and autonomously deployable by completely automated deployment machinery. There is a bare least of centralized management of these administrations, which may be written in various programming languages and utilize various data storage advancements.

As the turn to containerization and as microservices advance in an organization, they will before long need a strategy to maintain many containers and microservices. A few organizations will have hundreds or even thousands of containers running in the years ahead.

Future challenges

Life cycle forms alone are an important bit of operations and management. By what means will we automatically recuperate when a container fails? Which upstream administrations are affected by such an outage? By what means will we patch our applications with minimal vacation? In what capacity will we scale up our containers and administrations as our traffic develops?

Systems administration and handling are also important concerns. A few procedures are part of the same help and may profit by the closeness to the system. Databases, for example, may send large amounts of data to a particular microservice for handling. In what manner will we place containers near each other in our cluster? Is there regular data that should be accessed? In what capacity will new administrations be found and made available to other frameworks?

Resource utilization is also a key. The small impression of containers means that we can upgrade our infrastructure for greater utilization. Broadening the savings started in the elastic cloud will take us much further toward limiting wasted hardware. In what manner will we plan workloads most proficiently? In what manner will we guarantee that our important applications always have the correct resources? How might we run less important workloads on spare capacity?

Finally, portability is a key factor in moving many organizations to containerization. Docker makes it exceptionally easy to send a standard container across various operating frameworks, cloud suppliers, and on-premise hardware or even engineer laptops. Notwithstanding, despite everything we need tooling to move containers around. In what capacity will we move containers between various hubs on our cluster? By what method will we turn out updates with minimal disturbance? What procedure do we use to perform blue-green deployments or canary releases?

Whether you are starting to work out individual microservices and separating worries into isolated containers or in the event that you essentially want to take full advantage of the portability and immutability in your application advancement, the requirement for management and orchestration turns out to be clear. This is the place orchestration instruments, for example, Kubernetes offer the greatest value.

The introduction of Kubernetes

Kubernetes (K8s) is an open source venture that was released by Google in June, 2014. Google released the extend as part of a push to share their own infrastructure and innovation advantage with the network at large.

Google launches 2 billion containers seven days in their infrastructure and has been utilizing container innovation for over a decade. Originally, they were building a framework named Borg, presently called Omega, to plan their vast quantities of workloads across their consistently expanding data focus impression. They took many of the exercises they learned throughout the years and revamped their current data focus management apparatus for wide adoption by the remainder of the world. The outcome was the Kubernetes open-source venture (you can allude to more details about this in point 3 in the References area at the finish of the chapter).

Since its initial release in 2014, K8s has experienced rapid improvement with commitments all across the open-source network, including Red Hat,

VMware, and Canonical. The 1.0 release of Kubernetes went live in July, 2015. From that point forward, it's been a fast-paced advancement of the undertaking with wide help from one of the largest open-source networks on GitHub today. We'll be covering adaptation 1.5 all through the book. K8s gives organizations a device to deal with a portion of the major operations and management concerns. We will investigate how Kubernetes helps deal with resource utilization, high availability, updates, patching, organizing, administration disclosure, checking, and logging.

Our first cluster

Kubernetes is upheld on a variety of platforms and OSes. For the examples in this book, I utilized a Ubuntu 16.04 Linux VirtualBox for my customer and Google Compute Engine (GCE) with Debian for the cluster itself. We will also take a brief take a gander at a cluster running on Amazon Web Services (AWS) with Ubuntu.

To save some cash, both GCP and AWS offer complementary plans and trial offers for their cloud infrastructure. It merits utilizing these free trials for your Kubernetes learning, if conceivable.

The greater part of the ideas and examples in this book should chip away at any installation of a Kubernetes cluster. To get more information on other platform arrangements, allude to the Kubernetes beginning page on the accompanying GitHub link:

http://kubernetes.io/docs/beginning aides/

To start with, how about we make sure that our condition is appropriately set up before we install Kubernetes.

Start by updating packages:

$ sudo apt-get update

Install Python and twist in the event that they are absent:

$sudo apt-get install python

$sudo apt-get install twist

Install the gcloud SDK:

$ twist https://sdk.cloud.google.com | bash

We should start another shell before gcloud is on our path.

Arrange your Google Cloud Platform (GCP) account information. This should automatically open a program from where we can sign in to our Google Cloud account and authorize the SDK:

$ gcloud auth login

On the off chance that you have issues with login or want to utilize another program, you can optionally utilize the - no-launch-program command. Reorder the URL to the machine and/or program of your decision. Sign in with your Google Cloud credentials and snap Allow on the consents page. Finally, you ought to get an authorization code that you can reorder back into the shell where the brief is waiting.

A default task ought to be set, yet we can confirm this with the accompanying command:

$ gcloud config list venture

We can alter this and set another default venture with this command. Make sure to utilize venture ID and not extend name, as pursues:

$ gcloud config set task <PROJECT ID>

We can discover our undertaking ID in the support at the accompanying URL:

https://console.developers.google.com/venture

Alternatively, we can list active ventures:

$ gcloud alpha undertakings list

Since we have our condition set up, installing the latest Kubernetes variant is done in a solitary advance, as pursues:

$ twist - sS https://get.k8s.io | bash

It may take a moment or two to download Kubernetes relying upon your association speed. Earlier forms would automatically call the kube-up.sh content and start constructing our cluster. In rendition 1.5, we should call the kube-up.sh content ourselves to launch the cluster. As a matter of course, it will utilize the Google Cloud and GCE:

$ kubernetes/cluster/kube-up.sh

After you run the kube-up.sh content, we will see many lines move past. How about we take a gander at them each area in turn:

In the event that your gcloud segments are not cutting-edge, you may be provoked to update them.

The first image, GCE essential check, shows the checks for requirements as well as making sure that all segments are modern. This is explicit to each supplier. On account of GCE, it will confirm that the SDK is installed and that all segments are exceptional. If not, you will see a brief at this point to install or update:

Presently the content is turning up the cluster. Again, this is explicit to the supplier. For GCE, it first checks to make sure that the SDK is arranged for a default extend and zone. In the event that they are set, you'll see those in the yield.

Next, it uploads the server binaries to Google Cloud storage, as found in the Creating gs:...

lines:

It then checks for any bits of a cluster already running. Then, we finally start creating the cluster. In the yield in the previous figure Master creation, we see it creating the master server, IP address, and appropriate firewall configurations for the cluster:

Finally, it creates the flunkies or hubs for our cluster. This is the place our container workloads will actually run. It will continually circle and wait while all the followers start up. As a matter of course, the cluster will have four hubs (cronies), however K8s underpins having more than 1000 (and soon past). We will return to scaling the hubs later on in the book.

Presently that everything is created, the cluster is initialized and started. Assuming that everything goes well, we will get an IP address for the master. Also, note that configuration along with the cluster management credentials are put away in

home/<Username>/.kube/config:

Then, the content will validate the cluster. At this point, we are never again running supplier explicit code. The validation content will question the cluster via the kubectl.sh content. This is the central content for managing our cluster. In this case, it checks the quantity of followers found, enlisted, and in a ready state. It circles through surrendering the cluster to 10 minutes to complete initialization.

After a fruitful startup, a summary of the followers and the cluster segment health is imprinted on the screen:

Finally, a kubectl cluster-information command is run, which yields the URL for the master administrations including DNS, UI, and checking. We should take a gander at a portion of these segments.

Kubernetes UI

Open a program and run the accompanying code:

https://<your master ip>/ui/

The certificate is self-marked as a matter of course, so you'll have to overlook the warnings in your program before continuing. After this, we will see a login dialog. This is the place we utilize the credentials recorded during the K8s installation. We can discover them at any time by essentially utilizing the config command:

$ kubectl config see

The main dashboard takes us to a page with very little display from the beginning. There is a link to send a containerized app that will take you to a GUI for deployment. This GUI can be an extremely easy way to begin conveying apps without agonizing over the YAML syntax for Kubernetes. Be that as it may, as your utilization of containers matures, it's great practice to utilize the YAML definitions that are registered to source control.

On the off chance that you click on the Nodes link on the left-hand side menu, you will see a few measurements on the present cluster hubs:

At the top, we see an aggregate of the CPU and memory usages pursued by a posting of our cluster hubs. Tapping on one of the hubs will take us to a page with detailed information about that hub, its health, and various measurements.

The Kubernetes UI has a lot of other perspectives that will turn out to be increasingly valuable as we start launching real applications and adding configurations to the cluster.

Grafana

Another service installed as a matter of course is Grafana. This instrument will give us a dashboard to see measurements on the cluster nodes. We can access it utilizing the accompanying syntax in a program:

https://<your master

ip>/api/v1/intermediary/namespaces/kube-framework/services/observing grafana

From the main page, click on the Home dropdown and select Cluster. Here, Kubernetes is actually running various services. Heapster is utilized to gather the resource usage on the cases and nodes and stores the information in InfluxDB. The outcomes, for example, CPU and memory usage, are what we find in the Grafana UI. We will investigate this top to bottom in, Monitoring and Logging.

The kubectl content has commands to investigate our cluster and the workloads running on it. You can discover it in the/kubernetes/customer/ receptacle organizer. We will utilize this command all through the book, so we should take one moment to set up our condition. We can do as such by putting the binaries envelope on our PATH, in the accompanying manner:

$export PATH=$PATH:/<Path where you downloaded K8s>/kubernetes/ customer/canister

$chmod +x/<Path where you downloaded K8s>/kubernetes/customer/ canister

You may decide to download the kubernetes organizer outside your home envelope, so alter the first command as appropriate.

It is also a smart thought to make the changes permanent by adding the fare command as far as possible of your .bashrc document in your home index.

Since we have kubectl on our path, we can start working with it. It has many commands. Since we have not spun up any applications yet, a large portion of these commands won't be exceptionally intriguing. Be that as it may, we can investigate with two commands immediately.

In the first place, we have already observed the cluster-data command during initialization, yet we can run it again at any time with the accompanying command:

$ kubectl cluster-data

Another valuable command is get. It tends to be utilized to see as of now running services, cases, replication controllers, and much more. Here are the three examples that are helpful right out of the gate:

List the nodes in our cluster:

$ kubectl get nodes

List cluster occasions:

$ kubectl get occasions

Finally, we can perceive any services that are running in the cluster, as pursues:

$ kubectl get services

To start with, we will just observe one service, named kubernetes. This service is the center API server for the cluster.

Services running on the master

We should delve somewhat more profound into our new cluster and its center services. As a matter of course, machines are named with the kubernetes-prefix. We can adjust this utilizing

$KUBE_GCE_INSTANCE_PREFIX before a cluster is spun up. For the cluster we just started, the master ought to be named kubernetes-master. We can utilize the gcloud command-line utility to SSH into the machine. The accompanying command will start a SSH session with the master hub. Make certain to substitute your venture ID and zone to match your condition.

Also, note that you can launch SSH from the Google Cloud comfort utilizing the accompanying

syntax:

$ gcloud figure ssh - zone "<your gce zone>" "kubernetes-master"

On the off chance that you have issue with SSH via the Google Cloud CLI, you can utilize the Console which has a worked in SSH customer. Just go to the VM instances page and you'll consider a To be choice as a segment in the kubernetes-master listing. Alternatively, the VM instance details page has the SSH choice at the top.

When we are signed in, we ought to get a standard shell brief. How about we run the docker command that channels for Image and Status:

```
$ sudo docker ps - format 'table {{.Image}}t{{.Status}}'
```

Despite the fact that we have not conveyed any applications on Kubernetes yet, we note that there are several containers already running. Coming up next is a brief depiction of each container:

fluentd-gcp: This container gathers and sends the cluster logs record to the Google Cloud Logging service.

Hub issue finder: This container is a daemon that sudden spikes in demand for each hub and presently identifies issues at the hardware and part layer.

rescheduler: This is another add-on container that makes sure critical parts are always running. In cases of low resources availability, it may even expel less critical cases to make room.

glbc: This is another Kubernetes add-on container that gives Google Cloud Layer 7 load balancing utilizing the new Ingress capability.

kube-addon-manager: This part is center to the expansion of Kubernetes through various add-ons. It also periodically applies any changes to

the/and so on/kubernetes/addons index.

etcd-void dir-cleanup: An utility to cleanup void keys in etcd.

kube-controller-manager: This is a controller manager that controls a variety of cluster capacities, guaranteeing accurate and modern replication is one of its vital jobs. Additionally, it screens, manages, and finds new nodes. Finally, it manages and updates service endpoints.

kube-apiserver: This container runs the API server. As we investigated in the Swagger interface, this RESTful API allows us to create, inquiry, update, and expel various segments of our Kubernetes cluster.

kube-scheduler: This scheduler takes unscheduled units and ties them to nodes based on the present planning algorithm.

etcd: This runs the etcd software worked by CoreOS, and it is an appropriated and steady key-value store. This is the place the Kubernetes cluster state is put away, updated, and recovered by various segments of K8s.

pause: This container is often alluded to as the case infrastructure container and is utilized to set up and hold the systems administration namespace and resource limits for each case.

I precluded the amd64 for many of these names to make this increasingly conventional.

The motivation behind the units remains the same.

To leave the SSH session, basically type exit at the brief.

In the following chapter, we will also show how a couple of these services cooperate in the main image, Kubernetes center architecture.

Services running on the flunkies

We could SSH to one of the flunkies, however since Kubernetes plans workloads across the cluster, we would not see all the containers on a solitary crony. Be that as it may, we can take a gander at the cases running on all the cronies utilizing the kubectl command:

$ kubectl get cases

Since we have not started any applications on the cluster yet, we don't perceive any cases. Notwithstanding, there are actually several framework cases running bits of the Kubernetes infrastructure. We can see these cases by indicating the kube-framework namespace. We will investigate namespaces and their significance later, however for the time being, the -namespace=kube-framework command can be utilized to take a gander at these K8s framework resources, as pursues:

$ kubectl get cases - namespace=kube-framework

We should see something similar to the accompanying:

etcd-void dir-cleanup-kubernetes-master

etcd-server-occasions kubernetes-master

etcd-server-kubernetes-master

fluentd-cloud-logging-kubernetes-master

fluentd-cloud-logging-kubernetes-flunky bunch xxxx

heapster-v1.2.0-xxxx

kube-addon-manager-kubernetes-master

kube-apiserver-kubernetes-master

kube-controller-manager-kubernetes-master

kube-dns-xxxx

kube-dns-autoscaler-xxxx

kube-intermediary kubernetes-follower bunch xxxx

kube-scheduler-kubernetes-master

kubernetes-dashboard-xxxx

l7-default-backend-xxxx

l7-lb-controller-v0.8.0-kubernetes-master checking influxdb-grafana-xxxx hub issue identifier v0.1-xxxx rescheduler-v0.2.1-kubernetes-master

The initial six lines should look familiar. A portion of these are the services we saw running on the master and will see bits of these on the nodes. There are a couple of additional services we have not seen at this point. The kube-dns alternative gives the DNS and service disclosure plumbing, kubernetes-dashboard-xxxx is the UI for Kubernetes, l7-default-backend-xxxx gives the default load balancing backend for the new Layer-7 load balancing capability, and heapster-v1.2.0-xxxx and observing inundation grafana give the Heapster database and UI to screen resource usage across the cluster. Finally, kube-intermediary kubernetes-crony bunch xxxx is the intermediary which guides traffic to the best possible backing services and units running on our cluster.

On the off chance that we did SSH into a random follower, we would see several containers that stumble into a couple of these units. A sample may resemble this image:

Again, we saw a similar range of services with teachers. The services we did not see with the teacher are:

kubedns: This container monitors Kubernetes endpoint services and resources and synchronizes changes in DNS searches.

kube-dnsmasq: This is another container that provides DNS caching.

Dnsmasq-metrics: provides a metrics report for clustered DNS services.

l7-defaultbackend: this is the default system used to manage the GCE L7 and Ingress load balance.

kube-proxy: this is a network and utility proxy for your cluster. This component ensures that service traffic is directed to where your workloads are running in the cluster. We will explore this in more detail later in the book.

Hits: This tank is for monitoring and analysis.

addon-resizer: this cluster tool is used to scale the container.

heapster_grafana: Uses and monitors resources.

heapster_influxdb: this time is the database for Heapster data.

Auto Scale Cluster: This cluster tool is used for scaling

of the container in proportion to the size of the cluster.

exechealthz: performs capsule health checks.

Again, I omitted amd64 for many of these names to make it more general. The purpose of the pods remains the same.

Separate the cluster

Well, this is our first cluster at GCE, but let's explore other providers. To simplify things, we need to eliminate the one we just created at GCE. We can disassemble the cluster with a simple command:

$ kube-down.sh

Work with other vendors

Kubernetes uses the GCE provider for Google Cloud by default. We can override this default by setting the KUBERNETES_PROVIDER environment variable.

Let's try to configure a cluster in AWS. Before you begin, you must install and configure the AWS Command Line Interface (AWS) on our behalf. The installation and configuration documentation for the AWS CLI can be found at the following links:

Installation documentation:

http://docs.aws.amazon.com/cli/latest/userguide/installing.html#instal l-bundle-other-os

Configuration documentation:

http://docs.aws.amazon.com/cli/latest/userguide/cli-chap-getting-start ed.html

So, this is a simple parameter of the environment variable, as follows:

$ export KUBERNETES_PROVIDER = aws

Again, we can use the kube-up.sh command to activate the cluster as follows:

$ kube-up.sh

As with GCE, the installation activity takes a few minutes. It will organize the files in S3 and create the corresponding instances, virtual private cloud (VPC), security groups, etc., in our AWS account. The Kubernetes cluster will then be configured and started. When everything is finished and started, we should see a cluster confirmation at the end of the result:

Note that the region in which the cluster was created is determined by

KUBE_AWS_ZONE environment variable. By default, it is set to west-2a (the region is derived from this availability zone). Even if a region is defined in your AWS CLI, it will use the region defined in KUBE_AWS_ZONE.

Again we go to SSH as a teacher. This time we can use the native SSH client. We will find the key files in / home / <name>> /.ssh:

$ ssh -v -i / home / <username> / ssh / kube_aws_rsa ubuntu @ <Your primary IP address>

We will use sudo docker ps—format 'table {{.Image}} t {{. Status}} 'for research

Containers in operation. We should see the following:

We see some of the same containers as our GCE cluster. However, several are missing. We see the basic components of Kubernetes, but lack the fluentd-gcp service, as well as some of the new tools as a node issue

detector, reprogrammer, glbc, cubes-addon-manager and etcd-empty-dir-cleanup. This reflects some subtle differences in the cube-up scenario between different public cloud providers. Finally, this is decided by the efforts of the large open Kubernetes community, but GCP often offers many of the latest features.

Elasticsearch and Kibana are configured for us by AWS providers. We can find Kibana's user interface using a URL with the following syntax:

https: // <your primary IP address> / api / v1 / proxy / namespace / kube-system / services / kibana-logging

As with the user interface, you will be prompted to enter the administrator credentials that you can obtain using the config command, as shown below:

$ Kubectl configuration view

You must configure your index during your first visit. You can leave default values and select @timestamp for the name of the Time field. Then click Create and you will be taken to the index settings page. From there, click the Discover tab at the top to explore the license plates:

Cluster reset

You just tested the cluster in AWS. For the rest of the book, I will base my examples on the GCE group. For a better experience, you can easily return to the GCE cluster.

Simply disassemble the AWS cluster as follows:

$ kube-down.sh

Then create a new GCE cluster using the following elements:

$ export KUBERNETES_PROVIDER = gce

$ kube-up.sh

Edit your Cube-up settings

It is interesting to know the parameters used for the kube-up.sh script. Each provider in kubernetes / cluster / folder has its own folder containing the config-default.sh script.

For example, kubernetes / cluster / aws / config-default.sh has default settings for using kube-up.sh with AWS. At the beginning of this script, you will see many of these defined values, as well as environment variables that can be used to override the default values.

In the following example, the ZONE variable is set for the script and uses an environment variable value called KUBE_AWS_ZONE. If this variable is not defined, it will use the default us-west-2a value:

ZONE = $ {KUBE_AWS_ZONE: -us-west-2a}

Understanding these settings will help you get the most out of your kube-up.sh script.

Kube-up.sh alternatives

The Kube-up.sh script is always a very convenient way to start using Kubernetes on the platform you choose. However, it is not perfect and can sometimes succeed when conditions are not.

Fortunately, since the creation of K8, several alternative methods have emerged for cluster creation. Two of these GitHub projects are KOP and cubes-aws. Although the latter is linked to AWS, both offer an alternative way to easily mount your new cluster:

https://github.com/kubernetes/kops

https://github.com/coreos/kube-aws

In addition, several managed services have been created, including Google Container Engine (GKE) and Microsoft Azure Container Service (ACS), which provide automated installation and some cluster operations. We will review a short demonstration in Chapter 12, Ready for Production.

Out of nowhere

Finally, there is the possibility of starting over. Fortunately, starting with version 1.4, the Kubernetes team focused on simplifying the cluster configuration process. To this end, they introduced kubeadm for Ubuntu 16.04, CentOS 7 and HypriotOS v1.0.1 +.

Let's take a quick look at how to create a cluster in AWS using the kubeadm tool.

Cluster configuration

We will first need to secure our main cluster and nodes. We are currently limited to the above mentioned operating systems and version. Additionally, it is recommended that you have at least 1 GB of RAM and connect all nodes to the network.

For this visit, we will need an instance of t2.medium (primary node) and three instances of size t2.mirco (nodes) in AWS. These examples have an expandable processor and are loaded with at least 1GB of RAM. We will need to create a master node and three working nodes.

We will also need to create cluster security groups. The following ports are required for the teacher:

Once you have these SGs, go ahead and create four instances (one t2.medium and three t2.mircos) using Ubuntu 16.04. If you are new to AWS, see the documentation for creating EC2 instances at the following URL:

http://docs.aws.amazon.com/AWSEC2/latest/UserGuide/ LaunchingAndUsingInsances.html

Be sure to identify the instance of t2.medium as the master and join the main security group. List the other three nodes and connect them to the security group.

These steps are adapted to the detailed procedures in the manual. For more information or to use the Ubuntu alternative, see https: // kub

ernetes.io/docs/getting-started-guides/kubeadm/.

Installation of Kubernetes components (kubelet and kubeadm)

Then we will need SSH in all four instances and install Kubernetes components.

As a root, do the accompanying in all four instances:

1. Update packages and install apt-transport-https package so we can download HTTPS from source:

$ apt-get update

$ apt-get install - y apt-transport-https

2. Install the Google Cloud Public Key:

$ twist - s https://packages.cloud.google.com/apt/doc/apt-key.gpg | adding apt key -

3. Then create a source list to download the Kubernetes package with your favorite proofreader:

$ vi/and so on/apt/sources.list.d/kubernetes.list

4. Utilize the accompanying as substance for this document and save it:

deb http://apt.kubernetes.io/kubernetes-xenial main

List 1-1. /and so forth/apt/sources.list.d/kubernetes.list

5. Update your feeds again:

apt-get update

▪ Install Docker and Kubernetes major segments:

$ apt-get install - y docker.io

$ apt-get the chance to install - y kubelet kubeadm kubectl kubernetes-cni

Set up a teacher

In the case you have recently chosen as a teacher, we will initialize the teacher.

Run the accompanying command again as root:

$ kubeadm init

Note that initialization can just be done once. In the event that you have issues, you will require one

reset.

Hub Union

After fruitful initialization, you will get a join command that nodes can utilize.

Duplicate this later for the joining procedure. It should resemble this:

$ kubeadm join - token = <a token> <primary IP address>

The token is utilized to authenticate the cluster nodes. So make certain to keep yourself in a safe place for future reference.

organizing

Our cluster will require a system layer for underground communications. Note that kubeadm requires a CNI-compatible system structure. You can discover a list of at present available add-ons here:

http://kubernetes.io/docs/admin/addons/

For our example, we will utilize calico. We should create calico parts in our cluster utilizing the accompanying yaml. For your benefit, you can download it here:

http://docs.projectcalico.org/v1.6/beginning/kubernetes/installation/have ed/kubeadm/calico.yaml

When you have this document in your master, create the parts with the accompanying command:

$ kubectl apply - f calico.yaml

Allow it a moment to run the installer, then list the solid shape framework nodes to check:

$ kubectl get cases - namespace = kube-framework

You ought to get a list similar to the accompanying with three new shape and finished task not appeared:

Join the gathering

Presently we have to execute the association command we recently duplicated, in each of our hub instances:

$ kubeadm join - token = <a token> <primary IP address>

When done, you ought to have the option to see all nodes of the host utilizing this command:

$ kubectl gets nodes

summary

We briefly survey the operation of containers and their adaptation to new models of microservice architecture. You should now have a superior understanding of how these two powers will require various operations and administrative tasks and how Kubernetes offers amazing features to address these difficulties. We create two unique clusters in GCE and AWS and investigate the startup content as well as some integrated features of Kubernetes. Finally, we take a gander at alternatives to the kube-up content and test the new kubeadm apparatus in AWS utilizing Ubuntu 16.04.

In the following segment, we will investigate the basic idea and abstractions gave by K8 to managing containers and groups of complete applications. We will also audit basic planning, service revelation, and health control.

2

Pods, Services, Replication Controllers, and

Labels

This chapter will cover the center Kubernetes develops, namely cases, services, replication controllers, replica sets, and labels. A couple of straightforward application examples will be incorporated to demonstrate each build. The chapter will also cover basic operations for your cluster. Finally, health checks and booking will be presented with a couple of examples.

This chapter will talk about the accompanying points:

Kubernetes overall architecture

Introduction to center Kubernetes develops, namely cases, services, replication controllers, replica sets, and labels

Understanding how labels can ease management of a Kubernetes cluster

Understanding how to screen services and container health

Understanding how to set up booking constraints based on available cluster resources

The architecture

Although, Docker brings a supportive layer of abstraction and tooling around container management, Kubernetes carries similar assistance to orchestrating containers at scale and managing full application stacks.

K8s climbs the stack giving us builds to deal with management at the application or service level. This gives us automation and tooling to guarantee high availability, application stack, and service-wide portability. K8s also allows better control of resource usage, for example, CPU, memory, and circle space across our infrastructure.

Kubernetes gives this more significant level of orchestration management by giving us key develops to join numerous containers, endpoints, and data into full application stacks and services. K8s also gives the tooling to manage the when, where, and what number of the stack and its parts:

we see the center architecture of Kubernetes. Most administrative interactions are done via the kubectl content and/or RESTful service calls to the API.

Note the ideas of the ideal state and actual state carefully. This is the key to how Kubernetes manages the cluster and its workloads. All the bits of K8s are constantly attempting to screen the current actual state and synchronize it with the ideal state characterized by the administrators via the API server or kubectl content. There will be times when these states don't match up, yet the framework is always attempting to accommodate the two.

Master

Essentially, master is the brain of our cluster. Here, we have the center API server, which maintains RESTful web services for questioning and characterizing our ideal cluster and workload state. It's important to take note of that the control pane just accesses the master to initiate changes and not the nodes legitimately.

Additionally, the master incorporates the scheduler, which works with the API server to plan workloads as units on the actual follower nodes. These cases incorporate the various containers that make up our application stacks. Of course, the basic Kubernetes scheduler spreads cases across the cluster and uses various nodes for matching unit replicas. Kubernetes also allows determining necessary resources for each container, so planning can be altered by these additional factors.

The replication controller/replica set works with the API server to guarantee that the right number of case replicas are running at any given time. This is exemplary of the ideal state idea. On the off chance that our replication controller/replica set is characterizing three replicas and our actual state is two duplicates of the case running, then the scheduler will be summoned to add a third unit some place on our cluster. The same is valid if there are such a large number of units running in the cluster at any given time. Along these lines, K8s is always pushing toward that ideal state.

Finally, we have etcd running as a dispersed configuration store. The Kubernetes state is put away here and etcd allows values to be watched for changes. Think about this as the brain's shared memory.

Hub (once in the past followers)

In each hub, we have a few parts. The kubelet interacts with the API server to update the state and to start new workloads that have been summoned by the scheduler.

Kube-intermediary gives basic load balancing and coordinates the traffic bound for explicit services to the best possible unit on the backend. Allude to the Services area later in this chapter.

Finally, we have some default cases, which run various infrastructure services for the hub. As we investigated briefly in the past chapter, the units incorporate services for Domain Name System (DNS), logging, and case health checks. The default case will run alongside our planned units on each hub.

In v1.0, flunky was renamed to hub, yet there are still remnants of the term follower in a portion of the machine naming contents and documentation that exists on the Web. For clarity, I've added the term flunky in addition to hub in a couple of places all through the book.

Center builds

Presently, we should jump somewhat more profound and investigate a portion of the center abstractions Kubernetes gives. These abstractions will make it easier to consider our applications and ease the weight of life cycle management, high availability, and planning.

pods

The pods allow you to keep connected containers close to the network and hardware infrastructure. Data can live near the application, so processing can be done without generating long delays due to network travel. Similarly, shared data can be stored in volumes split between multiple containers. The pods basically allow for the logical grouping of containers and parts of our applications.

Although pods can run one or more containers inside, the pad itself can be one of many running on a Kubernetes node (minion). As we will see, darkness gives us a logical group of containers into which we can then copy, plan, and balance service endpoints.

Example under

Let's look at the capsule in action. We will run the Node.js application in the cluster. You will need a GCE cluster for this; If you haven't started yet, check out our first cluster in Chapter 1, Introduction to Kubernetes.

Now, let's create a directory for our definitions. In this example, we will create a folder in the subfolders / sample books of our home directory:

$ mkdir book examples

$ cd book examples

$ mkdir 02_example

$ cd 02_example

Download the sample code

Sample code files can be downloaded from your account at http://www.packtpub.com for any Packt Publishing book you purchased. If you purchased the book elsewhere, visit http://www.packtpub.com/support and register to receive the files directly by email.

Use your favorite editor to create the following file:

apiVersion: v1

like: Under

metadata:

name: node-js-pod

Specifications:

tanks:

- name: node-js-pod

image: bits / apache: back ports:

- containerPort: 80

Listing 2-1: nodejs-pod.yaml

This file is named node-js-pod with the last bitnami / apache container running on port 80. We can confirm this with the following command:

$ kubectl create -f nodejs-pod.yaml

The output is as follows:

under "node-js-pod" created

This gives us the floor that guides the specified tank. We can see more information about the substrate by executing the following command:

$ kubectl describes pods / node-js-pod

You will see a lot of information, such as floor status, IP address, and even relevant log events. You will notice that the floor IP address is a private IP address. We cannot access directly from a local computer. Don't worry, because the kubectl exec command reflects the functionality of Docker execution. Once the floor is started, with this function we can execute the command in the floor:

$ kubectl exec node-js-pod - curl <private IP>

By default, this executes the command on the first container found, but you can select a specific one using the -c arguments.

After the command is executed, you should see the HTML code. We'll have a better view later in this chapter, but for now, we can see that our module is really working as expected.

labels

Labels give us a second level of categorization, which becomes very useful in terms of business and day-to-day management. Like tags, tags can also be used as a basis for service discovery and as a useful grouping tool for daily operations and administrative tasks.

Tags are simple key-value pairs. You will see them in subsystems, replication controllers, replica kits, services and more. The label serves as the selector and tells Kubernetes resources to collaborate on various operations. Think of it as a filtering option.

We will explore labels in more detail in this chapter, but first we will explore the three remaining constructs: services, replication controllers, and replica sets.

The container's afterlife

As Werner Vogels, CTO of AWS, famously said everything fails all the time; containers and cases can and will crash, become ruined, or maybe even simply get accidentally shut off by a cumbersome admin jabbing around on one of the nodes. Solid strategy and security practices like implementing least benefit curtail a portion of these episodes, yet involuntary workload slaughter happens and is essentially a fact of operations.

Fortunately, Kubernetes gives two truly valuable develops to keep this grave affair all cleaned up behind the curtains. Services and replication controllers/replica sets enable us to keep our applications running with little interference and graceful recuperation.

Services

Services allow us to abstract access away from the buyers of our applications. Utilizing a reliable endpoint, clients and other programs can access cases running on your cluster seamlessly.

K8s achieves this by making sure that each hub in the cluster runs an intermediary named kube-intermediary. As the name proposes, the activity of kube-intermediary is to intermediary communication from a service endpoint back to the comparing unit that is running the actual application.

Participation of the service load balancing pool is controlled by the utilization of selectors and labels. Units with matching labels are added to the list of candidates where the service forwards traffic. A virtual IP address and port are utilized as the section focuses for the service, and the traffic is then forwarded to a random unit on a target port characterized by either K8s or your definition document.

Updates to service definitions are observed and coordinated from the K8s cluster master and propagated to the kube-intermediary daemons running on each hub.

Right now, kube-intermediary is running on the hub have itself. There are plans to containerize this and the kubelet as a matter of course later on.

Replication controllers and replica sets

Replication controllers (RCs), as the name recommends, manage the quantity of nodes that a unit and included container images run on. They guarantee that an instance of an image is being run with the particular number of duplicates.

As you start to operationalize your containers and cases, you'll need a way to turn out updates, scale the quantity of duplicates running (both here and there), or basically guarantee that at least one instance of your stack is always running. RCs create a significant level mechanism to make sure that things are operating effectively across the whole application and cluster.

RCs are just charged with guaranteeing that you have the ideal scale for your application. You characterize the quantity of unit replicas you want running and give it a template for how to create new cases. Much the same as services, we will utilize selectors and labels to characterize a case's participation in a replication controller.

Kubernetes doesn't require the exacting behavior of the replication controller, which is ideal for long-running procedures. In fact, work controllers can be utilized for brief workloads which allow occupations to be rushed to a fulfillment state and are appropriate for batch work.

Replica sets, are another sort, as of now in Beta, that speak to an improved variant of replication controllers. Right now, the main distinction comprises of having the option to utilize the new set-based label selectors as we will find in the accompanying examples.

Our first Kubernetes application

Before we proceed onward, we should take a glance at these three ideas in real life. Kubernetes ships with various examples installed, however we will create another example from scratch to illustrate a portion of the ideas.

We already created a case definition record, however as you learned, there are many advantages to running our cases via replication controllers. Again, utilizing the book- examples/02_example envelope we made earlier, we will create some definition records and start a cluster of Node.js servers utilizing a replication controller approach. Additionally, we'll add an open face to it with a load-balanced service.

Utilize your favorite editorial manager to create the accompanying record:

apiVersion: v1

kind: ReplicationController

metadata:

name: hub js

labels:

name: hub js

spec:

replicas: 3

selector:

name: hub js

template:

metadata:

labels:

name: hub js

spec:

containers:

- name: hub js

image: jonbaier/hub express-info:latest ports:

- containerPort: 80

Listing 2-2: nodejs-controller.yaml

This is the main resource definition document for our cluster, so how about we take a more intensive look. You'll take note of that it has four first-level components (kind, apiVersion, metadata, and spec). These are regular among all top-level Kubernetes resource definitions:

Kind: This discloses to K8s the sort of resource we are creating. In this case, the sort is

ReplicationController. The kubectl content uses a solitary create command

for all kinds of resources. The advantage here is that you can easily create various resources of various kinds without the requirement for determining individual parameters for each sort. In any case, it necessitates that the definition documents can recognize what it is they are determining.

apiVersion: This essentially reveals to Kubernetes which rendition of the schema we are utilizing.

Metadata: This is the place we will give the resource a name and also indicate labels that will be utilized to search and choose resources for a given operation. The metadata component also allows you to create annotations, which are for the non-recognizing information that may be helpful for customer apparatuses and libraries.

Finally, we have spec, which will vary based on the sort or kind of resource we are creating. In this case, it's ReplicationController, which guarantees the ideal number of units are running. The replicas component characterizes the ideal number of units, the selector component advises the controller which cases to watch, and finally, the template component characterizes a template to launch another case. The template segment contains the same pieces we saw in our case definition earlier. An important thing to note is that the selector values need to match the labels values indicated in the unit template. Recollect that this matching is utilized to choose the units being managed.

Presently, how about we take a gander at the service definition:

apiVersion: v1

kind: Service

metadata:

name: hub js

labels:

name: hub js

spec:

type: LoadBalancer

ports:

- port: 80 selector:

name: hub js

Listing 2-3: nodejs-rc-service.yaml

The YAML here is similar to ReplicationController. The main contrast is found in the service spec component. Here, we characterize the Service type, listening port, and selector, which tell the Service intermediary which units can answer the service.

Kubernetes bolsters both YAML and JSON formats for definition documents.

Create the Node.js express replication controller:

$ kubectl create - f nodejs-controller.yaml

The yield is as per the following:

replicationcontroller "hub js" created

This gives us a replication controller that guarantees that three duplicates of the container are always running:

$ kubectl create - f nodejs-rc-service.yaml

The yield is as per the following:

service "hub js" created

On GCE, this will create an external load balancer and forwarding rules, however you may need to add additional firewall rules. In my case, the firewall was already open for port 80. Be that as it may, you may need to open this port, especially in the event that you convey a service with ports other than 80 and 443.

Alright, presently we have a running service, which means that we can access the Node.js servers from a reliable URL. We should take a glance at our running services:

$ kubectl get services

In the first image (Services listing), we should take note of that the hub js service is

running, and in the IP(S) segment, we ought to have both a private and an open

(130.211.186.84 in the screen capture) IP address. In the event that you don't see the external IP, you may need to wait a moment for the IP to be allocated from GCE. How about we check whether we can associate by

opening up people in general address in a program:

You should see something like the figure Container data application . In the event that we visit on numerous occasions, you should take note of that the container name changes. Essentially, the service load balancer is rotating between available units on the backend.

Programs usually cache pages, so to really observe the container name change, you may need to clear your cache or utilize an intermediary like this one:

https://hide.me/en/intermediary

How about we take a stab at playing chaos monkey a piece and murder off a couple of containers to perceive what Kubernetes does. So as to do this, we have to see where the cases are actually running. To start with, how about we list our cases:

$ kubectl get cases

Presently, how about we get some more details on one of the cases running a hub js container. You can do this with the depict command with one of the case names listed in the last command:

$ kubectl depict unit/hub js-sjc03

You should see the first yield. The information we need is the Node: area. How about we utilize the hub name to SSH (short for Secure Shell) into the (follower) hub running this workload:

$gcloud process - venture "<Your venture ID>" ssh - zone "<your gce zone>" "<Node from

case describe>"

Once SSHed into the hub, on the off chance that we run a sudo docker ps command, we should see at least two containers: one running the pause image and one running the actual hub express-data image. You may see more if the K8s booked more than one replica on this hub.

How about we grab the container ID of the jonbaier/hub express-information image (not gcr.io/google_containers/pause) and slaughter it off to perceive what happens. Save this container ID some place for later:

$ sudo docker ps - filter="name=node-js"

$sudo docker stop <node-express container id>

$sudo docker rm <container id>

$sudo docker ps - filter="name=node-js"

Except if you are really fast you'll probably take note of that there is as yet a hub express-data container running, yet look carefully and you'll take note of that the container id is extraordinary and the creation time stamp shows just a couple of moments ago. On the off chance that you return to the service URL, it is working as normal. Feel free to leave the SSH session until further notice.

Here, we are already observing Kubernetes playing the job of on-call operations guaranteeing that our application is always running.

We should check whether we can discover any proof of the outage. Go to the Events page in the Kubernetes UI. You can discover it by navigating to the Nodes page on the main K8s dashboard. Select a hub from the list (the same one that we SSHed into) and look down to Events on the hub details page.

You should see three late occasions. Initially, Kubernetes pulls the image. Second, it creates another container with the pulled image. Finally, it starts that container again. You'll take note of that, from the time stamps, this all happens in under a second. Time taken may vary based on the cluster measure and image pulls, yet the recuperation is exceptionally brisk.

You may notice that if you open your browser in the direction of the load balancer, the load balancer always responds with the page. You can find the IP address of the load management tool using the kubectl get services command.

This happens for several reasons. First, the status check fails not only because / status does not exist, but the page on which the service shows still works normally between restarts. Second, livenessProbe is only responsible for restarting the tank during a state control failure. There is a separate preparation probe that will remove the container from the endpoint group in the answer service under.

Let's change the status control of a page that exists in our container to get proper status control. We will also add an availability check and refer it to a nonexistent status page. Open the nodejs-health-controller.yaml file and edit the specifications section

Match List 2-8 and save it as nodejs-health-controller-2.yaml:

apiVersion: v1

Type: ReplicationController

metadata:

name: node-js

tags:

name: node-js

Specifications:

Replicas: 3

selector:

name: node-js

Model:

metadata:

tags:

name: node-js

Specifications:

tanks:

- name: node-js

image: jonbaier / node-express-info: last

connectors:

- containerPort: 80 living spaces:

HTTP httpGet status check:

way: /

Port: 80 InitialDelaySeconds: 30 timeoutSeconds: 1

readinessProbe:

HTTP httpGet status check:

route: / country /

Port: 80 InitialDelaySeconds: 30 timeoutSeconds: 1

Example 2-8: nodejs-health-controller-2.yaml

This time, we will remove the old RC that kills the pods and create a new RC with our updated YAML file:

$ kubectl remove rc -l name = node-js

$ kubectl create -f nodejs-health-controller-2.yaml

Now, when we describe one of the pods, we only see the creation of pods and tanks. However, you will notice that the IP load balancer no longer works. If we execute the command described in one of the new nodes, we see an error message about the availability check, but the subkey continues to run. If we change the path of the free / busy probe: /, we can respond again to the main requests for service. Open nodejs-health-controller-2.yaml in the editor and make this update immediately. Then delete and recreate the replication driver:

$ kubectl remove rc -l name = node-js

$ kubectl create -f nodejs-health-controller-2.yaml

Now the IP load balancer should work again. Hold these modules as we will reuse them. Networks, load balancers and Ingress.

TCP controls

Kubernetes also supports status checks with simple TCP socket checks and also with custom command line scripts. The following fragments are examples of what two uses in a YAML file look like:

livenessProbe:

executive:

order:

- / usr / bin / health / checkHttpServce.sh

initialDelaySeconds: 90

timeoutSeconds: 1

Listing 2-9: Health Check Using Command Line Script

livenessProbe:

TCPSocket:

port: 80

initialDelaySeconds: 15

timeoutSeconds: 1

Sheets 2-10: Status Checking Using a Simple TCP Socket

Life cycle hook or smart stop

When you encounter problems in real-life scenarios, you may need to take additional action before closing the container or shortly after starting it. Kubernetes actually provides lifecycle hooks for these types of uses.

The following controller definition example defines an action after startup and an action before stopping before Kubernetes moves the container to the next phase of its life cycle.

apiVersion: v1

Type: ReplicationController

metadata:

name: apache hook

tags:

name: apache hook

Specifications:

Replicas: 3

selector:

name: apache hook

Model:

metadata:

tags:

name: apache hook

Specifications:

tanks:

- name: apache-hook

image: bits / apache: back ports:

- containerPort: 80 life cycle:

poststart:

HttpGet:

path: http://my.registration-server.com/register/

port: 80

pre-stop:

executive:

command: ["/ usr / local / bin / apachectl", "- k", "graceful-stop"]

More on labels

As referenced beforehand, labels are simply basic key-value pairs. They are available on cases, replication controllers, replica sets, services, and more. In the event that you recall our service YAML, in Listing 2-3: nodejs-rc-service.yaml, there was a selector attribute. The selector attribute reveals to Kubernetes which labels to use in discovering cases to forward traffic for that service.

K8s allows clients to work with labels straightforwardly on replication controllers, replica sets, and services. How about we alter our replicas and services to incorporate a couple of more labels. Indeed, utilize your favorite editorial manager and create these two records, as pursues:

apiVersion: v1

kind: ReplicationController

metadata:

name: hub js-labels

labels:

name: hub js-labels

app: hub js-express

deployment: test

spec:

replicas: 3

selector:

name: hub js-labels

app: hub js-express

```yaml
deployment: test
template:
metadata:
labels:
name: hub js-labels
app: hub js-express
deployment: test
spec:
containers:
- name: hub js-labels
image: jonbaier/hub express-info:latest ports:
- containerPort: 80
```

Listing 2-4: nodejs-labels-controller.yaml

```yaml
apiVersion: v1
kind: Service
metadata:
name: hub js-labels
labels:
name: hub js-labels
app: hub js-express
deployment: test
spec:
```

type: LoadBalancer

ports:

- port: 80 selector:

name: hub js-labels

app: hub js-express

deployment: test

Listing 2-5: nodejs-labels-service.yaml

Create the replication controller and service as pursues:

$ kubectl create - f nodejs-labels-controller.yaml

$ kubectl create - f nodejs-labels-service.yaml

How about we have a go at searching for replicas with test deployments:

$ kubectl get rc - l deployment=test

The accompanying screen capture is the aftereffect of the former command:

You'll see that it just returns the replication controller we just started. What about services with a label named segment? Utilize the accompanying command:

$ kubectl get services - l part

The accompanying screen capture is the aftereffect of the first command:

Here, we see the center Kubernetes service as it were. Finally, allows simply get the hub js servers we started in this chapter. See the accompanying command:

$ kubectl get services - l "name in (hub js,node-js-labels)"

Additionally, we can perform management tasks across various cases and services. For example, we can murder all replication controllers that are part of the demo deployment (in the event that we had any running), as pursues:

$ kubectl erase rc - l deployment=demo

Otherwise, murder all services that are part of a creation or test deployment (again, on the off chance that we had any running), as pursues:

$ kubectl erase service - l "deployment in (test, generation)"

It's important to take note of that, while label choice is very useful in day-to-day management tasks, it requires appropriate deployment cleanliness on our part. We have to make sure that we have a tagging standard and that it is actively followed in the resource definition records for all that we run on Kubernetes.

While we utilized service definition YAML records to create our services so far, you can actually create them utilizing a kubectl command as it were. To give this a shot, first run the get cases command and get one of the hub js case names. Next, utilize the accompanying open command to create a service endpoint for simply that case:

$ kubectl uncover units hub js-gxkix - port=80 - name=testing-celebrity - create-external-load-balancer=true

This will create a service named testing-celebrity and also an open celebrity (load balancer IP) that can be utilized to access this unit over port 80.

There are number of other optional parameters that can be utilized. These can be found with the accompanying command:

kubectl uncover - help

Replica sets

As examined earlier, replica sets are the better than ever form of replication controllers. They take advantage of set-based label choice, yet they are as yet thought to be beta at time of this composition.

This is an example of a ReplicaSet based on and similar to the ReplicationController in listing 2.4:

```
apiVersion: augmentations/v1beta1

kind: ReplicaSet

metadata:

name: hub js-rs

spec:

replicas: 3

selector:

matchLabels:

app: hub js-express

deployment: test

matchExpressions:

- {key: name, operator: In, values: [node-js-rs]}

template:

metadata:

labels:

name: hub js-rs

app: hub js-express

deployment: test

spec:

containers:
```

- name: hub js-rs

image: jonbaier/hub express-info:latest ports:

- containerPort: 80

Listing 2-6: nodejs-labels-replicaset.yaml

Health checks

Kubernetes gives two layers of health checking. To start with, as HTTP or TCP checks, K8s can attempt to interface with a particular endpoint and give a status of healthy on an effective association. Second, application-explicit health checks can be performed utilizing command-line contents.

How about we take a gander at a couple of health checks in real life. In the first place, we'll create another controller with a health check:

apiVersion: v1

kind: ReplicationController

metadata:

name: hub js

labels:

name: hub js

spec:

replicas: 3

selector:

name: hub js

template:

metadata:

labels:

name: hub js

spec:

containers:

- name: hub js

image: jonbaier/hub express-info:latest ports:

- containerPort: 80

livenessProbe:

An HTTP health check httpGet:

path:/status/

port: 80 initialDelaySeconds: 30 timeoutSeconds: 1

Listing 2-7: nodejs-health-controller.yaml

Note the addition of the livenessprobe component. This is our center health check component. From here, we can indicate httpGet, tcpScoket, or executive. In this example, we use httpGet to play out a straightforward check for a URI on our container. The test will check the path and port determined and restart the unit in the event that it doesn't effectively return.

Status codes somewhere in the range of 200 and 399 are all viewed as healthy by the test.

Finally, initialDelaySeconds gives us the adaptability to delay health checks until the unit has got done with initializing. The timeoutSeconds value is basically the break value for the test.

We should utilize our new health registration controller to replace the old hub js RC. We can do this utilizing the replace command, which will replace the replication controller definition:

$ kubectl replace - f nodejs-health-controller.yaml

Replacing the RC all alone won't replace our containers because despite everything it has three healthy cases from our first run. How about we execute off those units and let the updated ReplicationController replace them with containers that have health checks:

$ kubectl erase cases - l name=node-js

Presently, after waiting a moment or two, we can list the cases in a RC and grab one of the case

IDs to review somewhat more profound with the portray command:

$ kubectl depict rc/hub js

Presently, utilize the accompanying command for one of the cases:

$ kubectl portray units/hub js-7esbp

At the top, we will see the overall unit details. Contingent upon your planning, under State, it will either show Running or Waiting with a CrashLoopBackOff reason and some blunder information. A piece underneath that we can see information on our Liveness test and we will probably observe a failure check above 0. Further down we have the unit occasions. Again, contingent upon your planning, you are probably going to have various occasions for the unit. Inside a moment or two, you'll note a pattern of murdering, started, and created occasions repeating again and again. You ought to also observe a note in the Killing passage that the container is unhealthy. This is our health check failing because we don't have a page reacting at/status.

Listing 2-11: apache-snares controller.yaml

You'll note for the postStart snare, we characterize a httpGet action, yet for the preStop snare, I characterize an executive action. Similarly as with our health checks, the httpGet action attempts to make a HTTP call to the particular endpoint and port combination, while the executive action runs a local command in the container.

The httpGet and executive actions are both upheld for the postStart and preStop snares. On account of preStop, a parameter named reason will be sent to the handler as a parameter. See the accompanying table for valid values:

Note that snare calls are conveyed at least once. Therefore, any rationale in the action ought to gracefully handle different calls. Another important note is that postStart runs before a case enters its ready state. On the off chance that the snare itself fails, the case will be viewed as unhealthy.

Application planning

Since we understand how to run containers in units and even recuperate from failure, it may be helpful to understand how new containers are planned on our cluster nodes.

As referenced earlier, the default behavior for the Kubernetes scheduler is to spread container replicas across the nodes in our cluster. In the absence of all other constraints, the scheduler will place new cases on nodes with the least number of other cases having a place with matching services or replication controllers.

Additionally, the scheduler gives the ability to add constraints based on resources available to the hub. Today, this incorporates least CPU and memory allocations. Regarding Docker, these utilization the CPU-shares and memory limit flags under the spreads.

At the point when additional constraints are characterized, Kubernetes will check a hub for available resources. In the event that a hub doesn't meet all the constraints, it will move to the following. In the event that no nodes can be discovered that meet the criteria, then we will see a booking blunder in the logs.

The Kubernetes roadmap also has plans to help networking and storage. Because planning is such an important bit of overall operations and management for containers, we ought to hope to consider many to be in this area as the undertaking develops.

Booking example

How about we take a glance at a brisk example of setting some resource limits. On the off chance that we take a gander at our K8s dashboard, we can get a brisk snapshot of the present state of resource usage on our cluster

utilizing https://<your master

ip>/api/v1/intermediary/namespaces/kube-framework/services/ kubernetes-dashboard and tapping on Nodes on the left-hand side menu.

This view shows the aggregate CPU and memory across the entire cluster, nodes, and master. In this case, we have fairly low CPU utilization, however a not too bad lump of memory being used.

How about we see what happens when I attempt to turn up a couple of more units, yet this time, we will ask for

512Mi for memory and 1500 m for the CPU. We'll utilize 1500 m to determine 1.5 CPUs; since each hub just has 1 CPU, this should bring about failure. Here's an example of RC definition:

apiVersion: v1

kind: ReplicationController

metadata:

name: hub js-constraints

labels:

name: hub js-constraints

spec:

replicas: 3

selector:

```yaml
name: hub js-constraints
template:
metadata:
labels:
name: hub js-constraints
spec:
containers:
- name: hub js-constraints
image: jonbaier/hub express-info:latest ports:
- containerPort: 80 resources:
limits:
memory: "512Mi"
cpu: "1500m"
```

Listing 2-12: nodejs-constraints-controller.yaml

To open the first document, utilize the accompanying command:

```
$ kubectl create - f nodejs-constraints-controller.yaml
```

The replication controller finishes effectively, however on the off chance that we run a get units command, we'll note the hub js-constraints cases are stuck in a pending state. On the off chance that we look somewhat nearer with the depict cases/<pod-id> command, we'll note a booking blunder (for case id utilize one of the case names from the principal command):

```
$ kubectl get units
```

```
$ kubectl portray cases/<pod-id>
```

Note, in the base occasions segment, that the WarningFailedScheduling case blunder listed

in Events is accompanied by fit failure on node....Insufficient cpu after the

blunder. As you can see, Kubernetes couldn't locate a fit in the cluster that met all the constraints we characterized.

On the off chance that we currently adjust our CPU constraint down to 500 m, and then recreate our replication controller, we ought to have all three units running inside a couple of seconds.

Summary

We investigated the overall architecture for Kubernetes, as well as the center develops, gave to assemble your services and application stacks. You ought to have a superior understanding of how these abstractions make it easier to manage the existence cycle of your stack and/or services in general and not simply the individual segments. Additionally, we took a direct see how to manage some basic day-to-day tasks utilizing cases, services, and replication controllers. We also saw how to utilize Kubernetes to automatically react to outages via health checks. Finally, we investigated the Kubernetes scheduler and a portion of the constraints clients can determine to impact booking placement.

In the following chapter, we will plunge into the networking layer of Kubernetes. We'll perceive how networking is done and also take a gander at the center Kubernetes intermediary that is utilized for traffic directing. We will also take a gander at service disclosure and the logical namespace groupings.

Networking, Load Balancers, and Ingress

In this section, let us see how the Kubernetes cluster manages the network and how it differs from other approaches. We will describe the three requirements of Kubernetes network solutions and explore why they are necessary for easy operation. In addition, we will examine the problem for Kubernetes proxy services and work on each node. Finally, we will see a brief description of some of the characteristics of higher-level isolation across multiple organizations.

This chapter covers the following points:

Kubernetes Network

Advanced Services Concepts

Discovery service

DNS

Namespace restrictions and quotas

Kubernetes Network

Networking is a vital concern for manufacturing operations. At the service level, we need a reliable way for our application components to be located and communicate with one another. Introducing the container and grouping it into the mix of things make it more complicated, because now we need to consider a few name names. Communication and discovery become an exploit that must go beyond the container IP space, the host network, and sometimes even the network topologies of multiple data centers.

Kubernetes uses its origins in the sorting tools Google has used for the last ten years. Networking is an area where Google has outpaced the competition with one of the largest networks in the world. Previously, Google developed its hardware and software-defined network switches (SDNs) to give them greater control, redundancy, and efficiency in their daily network work (see paragraph 1 for more details). see the section at the end of the chapter for details). Several lessons learned from managing and networking two billion tanks a week were distilled to Kubernetes and served as the basis for the creation of K8 networks.

Networking in Kubernetes requires that each pod has its IP address. Implementation details may vary depending on the underlying infrastructure provider. However, all implementations must follow certain basic rules. First, and then Kubernetes does not allow the use of Network Address Translation (NAT) for container-to-node traffic or container-to-node traffic (minion). In addition, the IP address of the internal container must match the IP address used to communicate with it.

These rules preserve much of the complexity of the network suite and facilitate the design of applications. In addition, they eliminate the need to re-examine network communication in legacy applications migrated from existing infrastructure. Finally, in new applications, they enable larger scale management of hundreds and even thousands of applications and services.

K8s does this IP magic on a scale by using a placeholder. Remember that a paused container is often referred to as an infrastructure container pod, and it is your important task to reserve network resources for our application containers to run later. The pause container contains the network namespace and the IP of the entire basement and can be used by all running containers. The break container joins first and contains a namespace, while the next containers join as they begin.

Networking capabilities

Kubernetes offers a wide range of networking options. Some solutions work with native AWS and GCP layers. There are various overlapping complements, some of which will be addressed in the next section. Finally, the CNI (Container Networking Interface) plugins are compatible. CNI should be a common additional container architecture. It is currently compatible with several orchestration tools such as Kubernetes, Mesos and CloudFoundry. Discover more information about:

https://github.com/containernetworking/cni.

For a complete list of compatible network options, always consult the Kubernetes documentation.

Comparing networks

To better understand the container network, it might be instructive to consider alternative approaches to the container network. This following approaches do not make an exhaustive list, but should provide an overview of the options available.

Docker

The Docker Engine creates three sorts of systems as a matter of course. These are connected, host, and none.

The spanned system is the default decision except if generally determined. In this mode, the holder has its own systems administration namespace and is then crossed over by means of virtual interfaces to the host (or hub on account of K8s) arrange. In the connected system, two holders can utilize a similar IP extend in light of the fact that they are disconnected. Subsequently, administration correspondence requires some extra port mapping through the host side of system interfaces.

Docker likewise underpins a host arrange, which enables the holders to utilize the host organize stack. Execution is extraordinarily profited since it evacuates a degree of system virtualization; nonetheless, you lose the security of having a separated system namespace. Moreover, port use must be overseen all the more cautiously since all compartments share an IP.

At last, Docker underpins a none system, which creates a holder with no outer interface. Just a loopback gadget is appeared in the event that you investigate the system interfaces.

In every one of these situations, we are still on a solitary machine, and outside of a host mode, the holder IP space isn't accessible, outside that machine. Associating holders crosswise over two machines at that point requires NAT and port mapping for correspondence.

Docker client characterized systems

So as to address the cross-machine correspondence issue and permit more prominent adaptability, Docker likewise bolsters client characterized systems through system modules. These systems exist autonomous of the holders themselves. In this manner, compartments can join the equivalent existing systems. Through the new module engineering, different drivers can be accommodated different system use cases.

The first of these is the scaffold driver, which enables making of systems to some degree like the default connect organize.

The second is the overlay driver. So as to facilitate over numerous hosts, they should all concur on the accessible systems and their topologies. The overlay driver utilizes a dispersed key-esteem store to synchronize the system creation over numerous hosts.

Docker likewise underpins a Macvlan driver, which utilizes the interface and sub-interfaces on the host. Macvlan offers an increasingly proficient system virtualization and seclusion as it sidesteps the Linux connect.

The module system will permit a wide scope of systems administration potential outcomes in Docker. Actually, huge numbers of the outsider alternatives, for example, Weave have just created their very own Docker arrange modules.

Weave

Weave gives an overlay system to Docker holders. It tends to be utilized as a module with the new Docker arrange module interface, and it is additionally perfect with Kubernetes through a CNI module. In the same way as other overlay systems, many reprimands the presentation effect of the epitome overhead. Note that they have as of late included a review discharge with Virtual Extensible LAN (VXLAN) exemplification support, which enormously improves execution. For more data, visit

ast-datapath/.

Wool

Wool originates from CoreOS and is an etcd-supported overlay. Wool gives a full subnet to each host/hub empowering a comparable example to the Kubernetes practice of a routable IP for every unit or gathering of holders. Wool remembers a for bit VXLAN epitome mode for better execution and has a test multi-organize mode like the overlay Docker module. For more data, visit https://github.com/coreos/wool.

Undertaking Calico

Undertaking Calico is a layer 3-based systems administration model that uses the implicit steering elements of the Linux bit. Courses are engendered to virtual switches on each host by means of the Border Gateway Protocol (BGP). Calico can be utilized for anything from little scale sends to huge Internet-scale establishments. Since it works at a lower level on the system stack, there is no requirement for extra NAT, burrowing, or overlays. It can associate straightforwardly with the hidden system foundation. Moreover, it has helped to arrange level ACLs to give extra disconnection and security. For more data visit the accompanying URL:

http://www.projectcalico.org/.

Waterway

Waterway blends both Calico for arrange approach and Flannel for overlay into one arrangement. It underpins both Calico and Flannel type overlays and uses the Calico strategy requirement rationale. Clients can look over overlay and non-overlay alternatives with this arrangement as it consolidates the highlights of the former two undertakings. For more data visit the accompanying URL:

https://github.com/tigera/trench

Adjusted plan

It's essential to bring up the parity Kubernetes is attempting to accomplish by putting the IP at the case level. Utilizing special IP addresses at the host level is tricky as the number of compartments develops. Ports must be utilized to uncover benefits on explicit holders and permit outer correspondence. Moreover, the intricacy of running different administrations that could think about one another (and their custom ports) and dealing with the port space turns into a major issue.

Be that as it may, relegating an IP address to every holder can be pointless excess. In instances of sizable scale, overlay systems and NATs are required so as to address every holder. Overlay systems include inactivity, and IP locations would be taken up by backend benefits also since they have to speak with their frontend partners.

Here, we truly observe a preferred position in the deliberations that Kubernetes gives at the application and administration level. In the event that I have a web server and a database, we can keep them on a similar case and utilize a solitary IP address. The web server and database can utilize the nearby interface and standard ports to impart, and no custom arrangement is required. Further, benefits on the backend are not unnecessarily presented to other application stacks running somewhere else in the group (yet potentially on a similar host). Since the case sees a similar IP address that the applications running inside it see, administration disclosure doesn't require any extra interpretation.

On the off chance that you need the adaptability of an overlay arrange, you can at present utilize an overlay at the case level. Weave, Flannel, and Project Calico can be utilized with Kubernetes just as a plenty of different modules and overlays accessible at this point.

This is additionally extremely accommodating with regards to booking the remaining burdens. It is a key to have a basic and standard structure for the scheduler to coordinate requirements and understand where space exists on the group's system at some random time. This is a powerful situation with an assortment of uses and assignments running, so any extra multifaceted nature here will have undulating impacts.

There are additionally suggestions for administration disclosure. New administrations coming on the web must decide and enlist an IP address on which the remainder of the world, or possibly group, can contact them. In the event that NAT is utilized, the administrations will require an extra system to gain proficiency with their remotely confronting IP.

Propelled administrations

How about we investigate the IP technique as it identifies with administrations and correspondence between holders. In the event that you review, in the Services segment, Chapter 2, Pods, Services, Replication Controllers, and Labels, you discovered that Kubernetes is utilizing kube-intermediary to decide the correct unit IP address and port serving each solicitation. In the background, kube-proxy is really utilizing virtual IPs and iptables to make this enchantment work

Kube-proxy currently has two modes—userspace and iptables. Starting at now, 1.2 iptables is the default mode. In the two modes, kube-proxy is running on each host. Its first obligation is to screen the API from the Kubernetes ace. Any updates to administrations will trigger an update to iptables from kube-proxy. For instance, when another help is created, a virtual IP address is picked and a standard in iptables is set, which will guide its traffic to kube-proxy by means of a random port. Accordingly, we currently have an approach to catch administration ordained traffic on this hub. Since kube-proxy is running on all hubs, we have group wide goals for the administration VIP (short for virtual IP). Moreover, DNS records can point to this VIP also.

In the userspace mode, we have a snare created in iptables, yet the proxying of traffic is as yet handled by kube-proxy. The iptables rule is just sending traffic to the administration passage in kube-proxy now. Once kube-proxy gets the traffic for specific assistance, it should then advance it to a case in the administration's pool of candidates. It does this utilizing a random port that was chosen during administration creation.

It is likewise conceivable to constantly advance traffic from a similar client IP to the equivalent backend unit/compartment utilizing the sessionAffinity component in your administration definition.

In the iptables mode, the units are coded legitimately in the iptable guidelines. This evacuates the reliance on kube-proxy for really proxying the traffic. The solicitation will go directly to iptables and then on to the unit. This is quicker and expels a potential purpose of disappointment.

Outer administrations

In the past section, we saw a couple of administration models. For testing and exhibition purposes, we needed every one of the administrations to be remotely open. This was arranged by the sort: LoadBalancer component in our administration definition. The LoadBalancer type creates an outer burden balancer on the cloud supplier. We should take note of that help for outside burden balancers differs by supplier, as does the usage. For our situation, we are utilizing GCE, so coordination is quite smooth. The main extra arrangement required is to open firewall rules for the outer help ports.

How about we burrow somewhat more profound and do a portray command on one of the administrations from the Pods, Services, Replication Controllers, and Labels:

$ kubectl depict administration/hub js-names

In the yield, in the former figure, you'll note a few key components. Our Namespace: is

set to default, Type: is LoadBalancer, and we have the outer IP recorded under LoadBalancer Ingress:. Further, we see Endpoints:, which shows us the IPs of the units accessible to answer administration demands.

Interior administrations

How about we investigate different sorts of administrations we can convey. To start with, as a matter of course, administrations are just inside confronting. You can determine a kind of clusterIP to accomplish this, be that as it may, if no sort is characterized, clusterIP is the expected sort. How about we investigate a model; note the absence of the sort component:

apiVersion: v1

kind: Service

metadata:

name: hub js-inner

names:

name: hub js-inner

spec:

ports:

- port: 80 selector:

name: hub js

Posting 3-1: nodejs-administration internal.yaml

Utilize this leaning to create the administration definition file. You'll require a solid variant of the hub js RC (Listing 2-7: nodejs-wellbeing controller-2.yaml). As should be obvious, the selector coordinates on the units named hub js that our RC propelled in the anterior part. We will create the administration and then rundown the as of now running administrations with a channel:

$kubectl create - f nodejs-administration internal.yaml

$kubectl get administrations - l name=node-js-inner

As should be obvious, we have another help, however just a single IP. Further, the IP address isn't remotely open. We won't have the option to test the administration from an internet browser this time. Be that as it may, we can utilize the handy kubectl executive command and endeavor to associate from one of the different cases. You will require hub js-case (Listing 2-1: nodejs-pod.yaml) running. At that point, you can execute the accompanying command:

$ kubectl executive hub js-unit - twist <node-js-inside IP>

This enables us to run a docker executive command as though we had a shell in the hub js-case holder. It at that point hits the inward help URL, which advances to any cases with the hub js name.

On the off chance that everything is great, you ought to recover the crude HTML yield. In this way, you effectively created an inner just help. This can be valuable for backend administrations that you need to make accessible to different compartments running in your group, yet not open to the world on the loose.

Custom burden adjusting

The third kind of administration that K8s permits is the NodePort type. This sort enables us to uncover help through the host or hub (crony) on a particular port. In this manner, we can utilize the IP address of any hub (crony) and access our administration on the alloted hub port. Kubernetes will appoint a hub port as a matter of course in the scope of 3000-32767, however you can likewise determine your own custom port. In the model in Listing 3-2: nodejs-administration nodeport.yaml, we pick port 30001, as pursues:

apiVersion: v1

kind: Service

metadata:

name: hub js-nodeport

names:

name: hub js-nodeport

spec:

ports:

- port: 80

nodePort: 30001

selector:

name: hub js

type: NodePort

Posting 3-2: nodejs-administration nodeport.yaml

By and by, create this YAML definition file and create your administration, as pursues:

$ kubectl create - f nodejs-administration nodeport.yaml

You'll take note of a message about opening firewall ports. Like the outside burden balancer type, NodePort is uncovering your administration remotely utilizing ports on the hubs. This could be valuable if, for instance, you need to utilize your heap balancer before the hubs. How about we ensure that we open those ports on GCP before we test our new assistance.

From the GCE VM occurrence reassure, click on the subtleties for any of your hubs (followers). At that point click on the system, which typically defaults except if generally indicated during creation. In Firewall rules, we can include a standard by clicking Add firewall rule.

We would now be able to test our new help, by opening a program and utilizing an IP address of any hub (follower) in your bunch. The configuration to test the new assistance is as per the following:

http://<Minoion IP Address>:<NodePort>/

At last, the most recent form has included an ExternalName type, which maps a CNAME to the administration..

Cross-node proxy

Recollect that kube-proxy is running on every one of the nodes, along these lines, regardless of whether the unit isn't running there, the traffic will be given a proxy to the suitable host. Allude to the Cross-node traffic figure for a visual on how the traffic streams. A client makes a solicitation to an outside IP or URL. The solicitation is adjusted by Node for this situation. In any case, the case doesn't occur to run on this node. This isn't an issue in light of the fact that the case IP addresses are routable. Thus, Kube- proxy or iptables just passes traffic onto the unit IP for this administration. The system steering at that point finishes on Node 2, where the mentioned application lives:

Custom ports

Administrations additionally enable you to outline traffic to different ports; at that point the compartments and units uncover themselves. We will create a help that uncovered port 90 and advances traffic to port 80 on the units. We will call the node-js-90 unit to mirror the custom port number. Create the accompanying two definition files:

apiVersion: v1

kind: ReplicationController

metadata:

name: node-js-90

names:

name: node-js-90

spec:

copies: 3

selector:

name: node-js-90

layout:

metadata:

names:

name: node-js-90

spec:

compartments:

- name: node-js-90

picture: jonbaier/node-express-info:latest ports:

- containerPort: 80

Posting 3-3: nodejs-customPort-controller.yaml

apiVersion: v1

kind: Service

metadata:

name: node-js-90

names:

name: node-js-90

spec:

type: LoadBalancer

ports:

- port: 90

targetPort: 80

selector:

name: node-js-90

Posting 3-4: nodejs-customPort-service.yaml

You'll take note of that in the administration definition, we have a targetPort component. This component advises the administration the port to use for cases/holders in the pool. As we saw in past models, on the off chance that you don't determine targetPort, it accept that it's a similar port as the administration. This port is as yet utilized as the administration port, be that as it may, for this situation, we are going to uncover the administration on port 90 while the holders serve content on port 80.

Create this RC and administration and open the fitting firewall rules, as we did in the last model. It might pause for a minute for the outside burden balancer IP to proliferate to the get administration command. When it does, you ought to have the option to open and see our commonplace web application in a program utilizing the accompanying arrangement:

http://<external administration IP>:90/

Different ports

Another custom port use case is that of different ports. Numerous applications uncover various ports, for example, HTTP on port 80 and port 8888 for web servers. The accompanying model shows our application reacting on the two ports. By and by, we'll additionally need to include a firewall rule for this port, as we accomplished for Listing 3-2: nodejs-administration nodeport.yaml already:

apiVersion: v1

kind: ReplicationController

metadata:

name: node-js-multi

marks:

name: node-js-multi

spec:

imitations: 3

selector:

name: node-js-multi

format:

metadata:

marks:

name: node-js-multi

spec:

holders:

- name: node-js-multi

picture: jonbaier/node-express-multi:latest ports:

- containerPort: 80

- containerPort: 8888

Posting 3-5: nodejs-multi-controller.yaml

apiVersion: v1

kind: Service

metadata:

name: node-js-multi

marks:

name: node-js-multi

spec:

type: LoadBalancer

ports:

- name: http

convention: TCP

port: 80

- name: counterfeit administrator http

convention: TCP

port: 8888

selector:

name: node-js-multi

Posting 3-6: nodejs-multi-service.yaml

The application and holder itself must tune in on the two ports for this to work. In this model, port 8888 is utilized to speak to a phony administrator interface.

On the off chance that, for instance, you need to tune in on port 443, you would require a legitimate SSL attachment tuning in on the server.

Entrance

We talked about already how Kubernetes utilizes the administration unique as a way to proxy traffic to support case dispersed all through our bunch. While this is useful in both scaling and unit recuperation, there are further developed steering situations that are not tended to by this structure.

Keeping that in mind, Kubernetes has included an Ingress asset, which takes into account custom proxying and burden adjusting to a back help. Consider it an additional layer or bounce in the steering way before traffic hits our administration. Similarly as an application has a help and support cases, the Ingress asset needs both an Ingress passage point and an Ingress controller that play out the custom rationale. The passage point characterizes the courses and the controller really handles the directing. For our models, we will utilize the default GCE backend.

A few restrictions to know about when utilizing the Ingress API can be found here:

https://github.com/kubernetes/contrib/mass/ace/entrance/cont   rollers/ gce/BETA_LIMITATIONS.md

As you may review, in Chapter 1, Introduction to Kubernetes, we saw that a GCE group returns with a default which gives Layer 7 burden adjusting capacity. We can see this controller running on the off chance that we take a gander at the kube-system namespace:

$ kubectl get rc - namespace=kube-system

We should see a RC recorded with the l7-default-backend-v1.0 name

This gives the Ingress controller piece that really courses the traffic characterized in our Ingress section focuses. How about we create a few assets for an Ingress.

To begin with, we will create a couple of new replication controllers with my httpwhalesay picture. This is a remix of the first whalesay that was shown in a program. The accompanying posting shows the YAML. Notice the three runs that let us join a few assets into one YAML file:

```
apiVersion: v1

kind: ReplicationController

metadata:

name: whale-entrance a

spec:

reproductions: 1

format:

metadata:

marks:

application: whale-entrance a

spec:

holders:

- name: sayhey

picture: jonbaier/httpwhalesay:0.1

command: ["node", "index.js", "Whale Type A, Here."] ports:

- containerPort: 80

-

apiVersion: v1

kind: ReplicationController

metadata:
```

name: whale-entrance b

spec:

imitations: 1

format:

metadata:

marks:

application: whale-entrance b

spec:

holders:

- name: sayhey

picture: jonbaier/httpwhalesay:0.1

command: ["node", "index.js", "Hello man, It's Whale B, Just Chillin'."]

ports:

- containerPort: 80

Posting 3-7. whale-rcs.yaml

Notice that we are making cases with a similar holder, yet different beginning up parameters. Observe these parameters for some other time. We will likewise create Service endpoints for every one of these RCs:

apiVersion: v1

kind: Service

metadata:

name: whale-svc-a

marks:

application: whale-entrance a

spec:

type: NodePort

ports:

- port: 80

nodePort: 30301

convention: TCP

name: http

selector:

application: whale-entrance a

-

apiVersion: v1

kind: Service

metadata:

name: whale-svc-b

marks:

application: whale-entrance b

spec:

type: NodePort

ports:

- port: 80

nodePort: 30284

convention: TCP

name: http

selector:

application: whale-entrance b

-

apiVersion: v1

kind: Service

metadata:

name: whale-svc-default

marks:

application: whale-entrance a

spec:

type: NodePort

ports:

- port: 80

nodePort: 30302

convention: TCP

name: http

selector:

application: whale-entrance a

Posting 3-8. whale-svcs.yaml

Again create these with the kubectl create - f command, as pursues:

$kubectl create - f whale-rcs.yaml

$kubectl create - f whale-svcs.yaml

We should see messages about the RCs and Services fruitful creation. Next, we have to characterize the Ingress section point. We will utilize http://a.whale.hey and http://b.whale.hey as our demo passage focuses:

apiVersion: expansions/v1beta1

kind: Ingress

metadata:

name: whale-entrance

spec:

rules:

- host: a.whale.hey http:

ways:

- path:/backend:

serviceName: whale-svc-a

servicePort: 80

- host: b.whale.hey http:

ways:

- path:/backend:

serviceName: whale-svc-b

servicePort: 80

Posting 3-9. whale-ingress.yaml

Once more, use kubectl create - f to create this Ingress. When this is effectively created, we should sit tight a couple of seconds for GCE to give the Ingress a static IP address. Utilize the accompanying command to watch the Ingress asset:

$ kubectl get entrance

Since this is definitely not an enrolled space name, we should indicate the goals in the twist command, this way:

$ twist - resolve a.whale.hey:80:130.211.24.177 http://a.whale.hey/

We can likewise attempt the subsequent URL and we will get our second RC:

$ twist - resolve b.whale.hey:80:130.211.24.177 http://b.whale.hey/

We see that the images are nearly the equivalent, then again, actually the words from each whale mirror the startup parameters from each RC we began before. In this way our two Ingress indicates are coordinating traffic different backends.

In this model, we utilized the default GCE backend for an Ingress controller. Kubernetes enables us to manufacture our own and Nginx really has a couple of forms accessible too.

Movements, multicluster, and more

As you've seen up until now, Kubernetes offers an elevated level of adaptability and customization to create a help reflection around your compartments running in the group. Be that as it may, there might be times where you need to point to something outside your group.

A case of this would work with heritage systems or even applications running on another bunch. On account of the previous, this is a superbly decent system so as to relocate to Kubernetes and compartments all in all. We can start to deal with the administration endpoints in Kubernetes while sewing the stack together utilizing the K8s organization ideas. Also, we can even begin bringing once again bits of the stack, as the frontend, each in turn as the association refactors applications for microservices and/or containerization.

To enable access to non-case based applications, the administrations build enables you to utilize endpoints that are outside the bunch. Kubernetes is really making an endpoint asset each time you create an assistance that utilizations selectors. The endpoints object monitors the unit IPs in the heap adjusting pool. You can see this by running a get endpoints command, as pursues:

$ kubectl get endpoints

You should see something like this:

NAMEENDPOINTS

http-pd10.244.2.29:80,10.244.2.30:80,10.244.3.16:80

kubernetes10.240.0.2:443

node-js10.244.0.12:80,10.244.2.24:80,10.244.3.13:80

You'll take note of a section for every one of the administrations we as of now have running on our bunch. For most administrations, the endpoints are only the IP of each case running in a RC. As I referenced, Kubernetes does this naturally dependent on the selector. As we scale the reproductions in a controller with coordinating marks, Kubernetes will refresh the endpoints consequently.

On the off chance that we need to create a help for something that isn't a case and along these lines has no marks to choose, we can without much of a stretch do this with both an assistance and endpoint definition, as pursues:

apiVersion: v1

kind: Service

metadata:

name: custom-administration

spec:

type: LoadBalancer

ports:

- name: http

convention: TCP

port: 80

Posting 3-10: nodejs-custom-service.yaml

apiVersion: v1

kind: Endpoints

metadata:

name: custom-administration

subsets:

- addresses:

- ip: <X.X.X.X> ports:

- name: http

port: 80

convention: TCP

Posting 3-11: nodejs-custom-endpoint.yaml

In the previous model, you'll have to supplant <X.X.X.X> with a genuine IP address, where the new help can point to. For my situation, I utilized the general population load balancer IP from the node-js-multi administration we created before in posting 3-6. Feel free to create these assets now.

In the event that we presently run a get endpoints command, we will see this IP address at port 80 related with the custom-administration endpoint. Further, in the event that we take a gander at the administration subtleties, we will see the IP recorded in the Endpoints area:

$ kubectl portray administration/custom-administration

We can try out this new assistance by opening the custom-administration outside IP from a program.

Custom addressing

Another choice to customize administrations is with the clusterIP component. In our models up until now, we've not determined an IP address, which implies that it picks the inward address of the administration for us. In any case, we can include this component and pick the IP address ahead of time with something like clusterip: 10.0.125.105.

There might be times when you would prefer not to stack balance and would prefer to have DNS with A records for each unit. For instance, software that requirements to imitate information uniformly to all nodes may depend on A records to convey information. For this situation, we can utilize a model like the accompanying one and set clusterip to None. Kubernetes won't allot an IP address and rather just dole out A records in DNS for every one of the units. In the event that you are utilizing DNS, the administration ought to be accessible at node-js-none or node-js-none.default.cluster.local from inside the group. We have the accompanying code:

apiVersion: v1

kind: Service

metadata:

name: node-js-none

marks:

name: node-js-none

spec:

clusterIP: None

ports:

- port: 80 selector:

name: node-js

Posting 3-12: nodejs-headless-service.yaml

Test it out after you create this administration with the trusty executive command:

$ kubectl executive node-js-case - twist node-js-none

Administration disclosure

As we examined before, the Kubernetes ace monitors all help definitions and updates. Revelation can happen in one of three different ways. The initial two techniques use Linux condition factors. There is support for the Docker connect style of condition factors, yet Kubernetes additionally has its naming show. Here is a case of what our node-js administration model may look like utilizing K8s condition factors (note IPs will change):

NODE_JS_PORT_80_TCP=tcp://10.0.103.215:80

NODE_JS_PORT=tcp://10.0.103.215:80

NODE_JS_PORT_80_TCP_PROTO=tcp

NODE_JS_PORT_80_TCP_PORT=80

NODE_JS_SERVICE_HOST=10.0.103.215

NODE_JS_PORT_80_TCP_ADDR=10.0.103.215

NODE_JS_SERVICE_PORT=80

Posting 3-13: Service condition factors

Another alternative for disclosure is through DNS. While condition factors can be valuable when DNS isn't accessible, it has downsides. The system creates factors at creation time, so benefits that come online later won't be found or would require some extra tooling to refresh all the system situations.

DNS

DNS comprehends the issues seen with condition factors by enabling us to reference the administrations by their names. As administrations restart, scale out, or show up once more, the DNS sections will refresh and guaranteeing that the administration name consistently indicates the most recent framework. DNS is set up naturally in a large portion of the upheld suppliers.

On the off chance that DNS is bolstered by your supplier, yet not set up, you can arrange the accompanying factors in your default supplier config when you create your Kubernetes group:

ENABLE_CLUSTER_DNS="${KUBE_ENABLE_CLUSTER_DNS:-true}"

DNS_SERVER_IP="10.0.0.10"

DNS_DOMAIN="cluster.local"

DNS_REPLICAS=1

With DNS dynamic, administrations can be gotten to in one of two structures—either the administration name itself, <service-name> or a completely qualified name that incorporates the namespace, <service-name>.<namespace-name>.cluster.local. In our models, it would appear to be like node-js-90 or node-js-90.default.cluster.local.

Multitenancy

Kubernetes likewise has an extra build for confinement at the group level. By and large, you can run Kubernetes and never stress over namespaces; everything will run in the default namespace if not indicated. In any case, in situations where you run multitenancy networks or need wide scale isolation and detachment of the bunch assets, namespaces can be utilized to this end.

To begin, Kubernetes has two namespaces—default and kube-system. The kube-system namespace is utilized for all the system-level compartments

The UI, logging, DNS, and so on are altogether run in kube-system. Everything else the client creates runs in the default namespace. Be that as it may, our asset definition files can alternatively indicate a custom namespace. For testing, how about we investigate how to construct another namespace.

To start with, we'll have to create a namespace definition file like the one in this posting:

apiVersion: v1

kind: Namespace

metadata:

name: test

Posting 3-14: test-ns.yaml

We can feel free to create this file with our handy create command:

$ kubectl create - f test-ns.yaml

Presently we can create assets that utilization the test namespace. Coming up next is a case of a unit utilizing this new namespace:

apiVersion: v1

kind: Pod

metadata:

name: utility

namespace: test

spec:

holders:

- image: debian:latest command:

- sleep

- "3600"

name: utility

Posting 3-15: ns-pod.yaml

While the case can in any case get to administrations in different namespaces, it should utilize the long DNS

type of <service-name>.<namespace-name>.cluster.local. For instance, if you somehow managed to run a command from inside the holder in Listing 3-15: ns-pod.yaml, you could utilize node-js.default.cluster.local to get to the Node.js

Here is a note about asset use. Eventually in this book, you may come up short on space on your bunch to create new Kubernetes assets. The planning will fluctuate dependent on bunch size, however it's great to remember this and do some tidy up now and again. Utilize the accompanying commands to expel old models:

$ kubectl erase unit <pod name>

$ kubectl erase svc <service name>

$kubectl erase rc <replication controller name>

$kubectl erase rs <replicaset name>

Breaking points

We should examine our new namespace more. Run the depict command as pursues:

$ kubectl depict namespace/test

Kubernetes enables you as far as possible the assets utilized by singular cases or compartments and the assets utilized by the general namespace utilizing portions. You'll take note of that there are no asset points of confinement or shares at present set on the test namespace.

Assume we need to restrain the impression of this new namespace; we can set quantities, for example, the accompanying:

apiVersion: v1

kind: ResourceQuota

metadata:

name: test-shares

namespace: test

spec:

hard:

cases: 3

administrations: 1

replicationcontrollers: 1

Posting 3-16: quota.yaml

As a general rule, namespaces would be for bigger application networks and would most likely never have portions this low. I am utilizing this so as to ease outline of the ability in the model.

Here, we will create a portion of 3 cases, 1 RC, and 1 assistance for the test namespace. As you likely speculated, this is executed by and by our trusty create command:

$ kubectl create - f quota.yaml

Since we have that set up, how about we use portray on the namespace, as pursues:

$ kubectl depict namespace/test

You'll take note of that we presently have a few qualities recorded in the amount segment and the points of confinement segment is as yet clear. We likewise have a Used segment, which tells us how near the points of confinement we are right now. We should attempt to turn up a couple of units utilizing the accompanying definition:

apiVersion: v1

kind: ReplicationController

metadata:

name: busybox-ns

namespace: test

names:

name: busybox-ns

spec:

copies: 4

selector:

name: busybox-ns

layout:

metadata:

names:

name: busybox-ns

spec:

compartments:

- name: busybox-ns

picture: busybox command:

- sleep

- "3600"

Posting 3-17: busybox-ns.yaml

You'll take note of that we are making four copies of this essential case. In the wake of utilizing create to fabricate this RC, run the depict command on the test namespace again. You'll see that the used qualities for cases and RCs are at their maximum. Nonetheless, we requested four copies and just observe three cases being used.

How about we see what's going on with our RC. You may endeavor to do that with the command here:

kubectl depict rc/busybox-ns

Notwithstanding, on the off chance that you attempt, you'll be disheartened to see a not discovered message from the server. This is on the grounds that we created this RC in another namespace and kubectl accept the default namespace if not determined. This implies we have to indicate -namepsace=test with each command when we wish to get to assets in the test namespace.

We can likewise set the current namespace by working with the setting settings. To start with, we have to locate our present setting, which is found with the accompanying command:

$ kubectl config see | grep current-setting

Next, we can take that specific circumstance and set the namespace variable like the accompanying:

$ kubectl config set-setting <Current Context> - namespace=test

Presently you can run the kubectl command without the need to determine the namespace. Make sure to switch back when you need to take a gander at the assets running in your default namespace.

Run the command with the namespace indicated. In the event that you've set your current namespace as exhibited in the tip box, you can leave off the - namespace contention:

$ kubectl depict rc/busybox-ns - namespace=test

As should be obvious in the previous picture, the initial three cases were effectively created, however, our last one comes up short with the Limited to 3 cases blunder.

This is a simple method as far as possible for assets parceled out at a network scale. Significantly, you can likewise set amounts for CPU, memory, constant volumes, and privileged insights. Also, limits work along these lines to share, however they set the breaking point for each unit or holder inside the namespace.

A note on asset utilization

As a large portion of the models in this book use GCP or AWS, it very well may be exorbitant to keep everything running. It's additionally simple to come up short on assets utilizing the default group size, particularly on the off chance that you keep each model running. In this manner, you might need to erase more seasoned cases, replication controllers, reproduction sets, and administrations intermittently. You can likewise pulverize the bunch and recreate utilizing Chapter 1, Introduction to Kubernetes as an approach to bring down your cloud supplier bill.

Summary

We investigated systems administration and administrations in Kubernetes. You should now understand how organizing correspondences are structured in K8s and feel great getting to your administrations inside and remotely. We perceived how kube-proxy adjusts traffic both locally and across the group. Also, we investigated the new Ingress assets that permit us better control of approaching traffic. We additionally took a gander at how DNS and administration disclosure is accomplished in Kubernetes. We polished off with brisk take a gander at namespace and separation for multitenancy.

Updates, Gradual Rollouts, And Autoscaling

This part will expand upon the center ideas, which tell you the best way to turn out updates and test new highlights of your application with insignificant disturbance to up-time. It will cover the nuts and bolts of doing application refreshes, progressive rollouts, and A/B testing. Likewise, we will take a gander at scaling the Kubernetes bunch itself.

This section will talk about the accompanying subjects:

Application scaling

Moving updates

A/B testing

Application autoscaling

Scaling up your group

Since form 1.2, Kubernetes has discharged a Deployments API. Arrangements are the prescribed method to manage scaling and application refreshes going ahead. Be that as it may, it is as yet thought to be beta at the hour of composing this book, while moving updates has been steady for a few renditions. We will investigate moving updates in this part as a prologue to the scaling idea and then plunge into the favored technique for utilizing arrangements in the following section.

Model set up

Before we start investigating the different capacities incorporated with Kubernetes for scaling and updates, we will require another model condition. We are going to utilize a variety of our past holder picture with a blue foundation (allude to the v0.1 and v0.2 (next to each other) picture, later in this part, for an examination). We have the accompanying code:

apiVersion: v1

kind: ReplicationController

metadata:

name: node-js-scale

names:

name: node-js-scale

spec:

copies: 1

selector:

name: node-js-scale

layout:

metadata:

names:

name: node-js-scale

spec:

compartments:

- name: node-js-scale

picture: jonbaier/unit scaling:0.1 ports:

- containerPort: 80

Posting 4-1: unit scaling-controller.yaml

apiVersion: v1

kind: Service

metadata:

name: node-js-scale

names:

name: node-js-scale

spec:

type: LoadBalancer

sessionAffinity: ClientIP

ports:

- port: 80 selector:

name: node-js-scale

Posting 4-2: unit scaling-service.yaml

Create these administrations with the accompanying commands:

$kubectl create - f unit scaling-controller.yaml

$kubectl create - f unit scaling-service.yaml

The open IP address for the administration may pause for a minute to create.

Scaling up

After some time, as you run your applications in the Kubernetes bunch, you will locate that a few applications need more assets, while others can make do with less assets. Rather than evacuating the whole RC (and related units), we need a progressively consistent approach to scale our application all over.

Fortunately, Kubernetes incorporates a scale command, which is fit explicitly for this reason. The scale command works both with Replication Controllers and the new Deployments deliberation. For the present, we will investigate the use with Replication Controllers. In our new model, we have just a single copy running. You can check this with a get units command:

$ kubectl get cases - l name=node-js-scale

How about we take a stab at scaling that up to three with the accompanying command:

$ kubectl scale - replicas=3 rc/node-js-scale

In the event that all goes well, you'll just observe the scaled word on the yield of your terminal window.

Alternatively, you can determine the - current-reproductions banner as a confirmation step. The scaling will possibly happen if the real number of reproductions presently running matches this check.

Subsequent to posting our units by and by, we should now observe three cases running with a name like node-js-scale-XXXXX, where the X characters are a random string.

You can likewise utilize the scale command to decrease the quantity of imitations. In either case, the scale command includes or expels the vital case reproductions, and the administration naturally updates and parities across new or remaining imitations.

Smooth updates

The scaling of our application all over as our asset demands change is helpful for some creation situations, yet shouldn't something be said about basic application refreshes? Any generation system will have code updates, fixes, and highlight increments. These could be happening month to month, week by week, or even every day. Ensuring that we have a solid method to push out these progressions without interference to our clients is a vital thought.

By and by, we profit by the long stretches of experience the Kubernetes system is based on. There is a worked in help for moving updates with the 1.0 form. The moving update command enables us to refresh whole RCs or simply the fundamental Docker picture utilized by every reproduction. We can likewise determine an update interim, which will enable us to refresh each case in turn and hold up until continuing to the following.

We should take our scaling model and play out a moving update to the 0.2 adaptation of our holder picture. We will utilize an update interim of 2 minutes, so we can watch the procedure as it occurs in the accompanying manner:

$kubectl moving update node-js-scale - image=jonbaier/unit scaling:0.2 - update-period="2m"

You should see some content about making another RC named node-js-scale-XXXXX, where the X characters will be a random series of numbers and letters. Likewise, you will see the start of a circle that is beginning one imitation of the new form and expelling one from the current RC. This procedure will proceed until the new RC has the full tally of copies running.

In the event that we need to track with continuously, we can open another terminal window and utilize the get units command, alongside a name channel, to perceive what's going on:

$ kubectl get units - l name=node-js-scale

This command will channel for units with node-js-scale in the name. On the off chance that you pursue this giving the moving update command, you should see a few cases running as it creates new forms and expels the old ones individually.

The full yield of the past moving update

As should be obvious here, Kubernetes is first making another RC named node-js-

scale-10ea08ff9a118ac6a93f85547ed28f6. K8s then circles through individually,

making another case in the new controller and expelling one from the old. This proceeds until the new controller has the full copy tally and the bygone one is at zero. After this, the old controller is erased and the enhanced one is renamed with the first controller name.

On the off chance that you run a get cases command now, you'll see that the cases still all have a more extended name. On the other hand, we could have indicated the name of another controller in the command, and Kubernetes will create another RC and units utilizing that name. By and by, the controller of the old name basically vanishes in the wake of refreshing is finished. I prescribe that you indicate another name for the refreshed controller to maintain a strategic distance from perplexity in your unit naming down the line. A similar update command with this strategy will resemble this:

$kubectl moving update node-js-scale node-js-scale-v2.0 - image=jonbaier/ unit scaling:0.2 - update-period="2m"

Utilizing the static outer IP address from the administration we created in the main segment, we can open the administration in a program. We should see our standard holder data page. Be that as it may, you'll see that the title currently says Pod Scaling v0.2 and the foundation is light yellow:

It's important that, during the whole update process, we've just been taking a gander at cases and RCs. We didn't do anything with our administration, yet the administration is as yet running fine and now coordinating to the new form of our cases. This is on the grounds that our administration is utilizing mark selectors for enrollment. Since both our old and new imitations utilize similar marks, the administration has no issue utilizing the new cases to support demands. The updates are done on the units individually, so it's consistent for the clients of the administration.

Testing, discharges, and cutovers

The moving update highlight can function admirably for a straightforward blue-green sending situation. In any case, in a genuine blue-green arrangement with a heap of different applications, there can be an assortment of interdependencies that require top to bottom testing. The update-time frame command enables us to include a break banner where some testing should be possible, however this won't generally be agreeable for testing purposes.

Correspondingly, you may need fractional changes to continue for a more drawn out time and as far as possible up to the heap balancer or administration level. For instance, you may wish to run an A/B test on another UI highlight with a segment of your clients. Another model is running a canary discharge (an imitation for this situation) of your application on new foundation like a recently included bunch node.

How about we investigate an A/B testing model. For this model, we should create another help that utilizations sessionAffinity. We will set the liking to ClientIP, which will enable us to advance clients to the equivalent backend unit. This is a key on the off chance that we need a segment of our clients to see one adaptation while others see another:

apiVersion: v1

kind: Service

metadata:

name: node-js-scale-abdominal muscle

marks:

administration: node-js-scale-abdominal muscle

spec:

type: LoadBalancer

ports:

- port: 80 sessionAffinity: ClientIP selector:

administration: node-js-scale-abdominal muscle

Posting 4-3: case AB-service.yaml

Create this administration as normal with the create command, as pursues:

$ kubectl create - f case AB-service.yaml

This will create a help that will point to our cases running both adaptation 0.2 and 0.3 of the application. Next, we will create the two RCs that create two copies of the application. One set will have form 0.2 of the application, and the other will have adaptation 0.3, as appeared here:

apiVersion: v1

kind: ReplicationController

metadata:

name: node-js-scale-a

names:

name: node-js-scale-a

form: "0.2"

administration: node-js-scale-stomach muscle

spec:

copies: 2

selector:

name: node-js-scale-a

version: "0.2"

service: node-js-scale-ab

template:

metadata:

labels:

name: node-js-scale-a

version: "0.2"

service: node-js-scale-ab

spec:

containers:

-name: node-js-scale

image: jonbaier/pod-scaling:0.2 ports:

-containerPort: 80 livenessProbe:

#An HTTP health check httpGet:

path: /

port: 80

initialDelaySeconds: 30

timeoutSeconds: 5

readinessProbe:

#An HTTP health check httpGet:

path: /

port: 80 initialDelaySeconds: 30 timeoutSeconds: 1

Listing 4-4: pod-A-controller.yaml

apiVersion: v1

kind: ReplicationController

metadata:

name: node-js-scale-b

labels:

name: node-js-scale-b

version: "0.3"

service: node-js-scale-ab

spec:

replicas: 2

selector:

name: node-js-scale-b

version: "0.3"

service: node-js-scale-ab

template:

metadata:

labels:

name: node-js-scale-b

version: "0.3"

service: node-js-scale-ab

spec:

containers:

-name: node-js-scale

image: jonbaier/pod-scaling:0.3 ports:

- containerPort: 80 livenessProbe:

#An HTTP wellbeing check httpGet:

way:/

port: 80

initialDelaySeconds: 40

timeoutSeconds: 6

readinessProbe:

#An HTTP wellbeing check httpGet:

way:/

port: 80 initialDelaySeconds: 30 timeoutSeconds: 1

Posting 4-5: unit B-controller.yaml

Note that we have a similar assistance mark, so these imitations will likewise be added to the administration pool dependent on this selector. We likewise have livenessProbe and readinessProbe characterized to ensure that our new form is functioning true to form. Once more, utilize the create command to turn up the controller:

$kubectl create - f unit A-controller.yaml

$kubectl create - f unit B-controller.yaml

Presently we have an assistance adjusting to the two adaptations of our application. In a genuine A/B test, we would now need to begin gathering measurements on the visit to every adaptation. Once more, we have sessionAffinity set to ClientIP, so all solicitations will go to a similar case. A few clients will see v0.2, and some will see v0.3.

Since we have sessionAffinity turned on, your test will probably show a similar form without fail. This is normal, and you would need to endeavor an association from different IP delivers to see both client encounters with every form.

Since the adaptations are each alone case, one can without much of a stretch separate logging and even add a logging holder to the case definition for a sidecar logging design. For quickness, we won't cover that arrangement in this book,

We can begin to perceive how this procedure will be helpful for a canary discharge or a manual blue-green organization. We can likewise perceive that it is so natural to dispatch another variant and gradually change over to the new discharge.

How about we take a gander at an essential change rapidly. It's truly as straightforward as a couple of scale commands, which are as per the following:

$kubectl scale - replicas=3 rc/node-js-scale-b

$kubectl scale - replicas=1 rc/node-js-scale-a

$kubectl scale - replicas=4 rc/node-js-scale-b

$kubectl scale - replicas=0 rc/node-js-scale-a

Utilize the get cases command joined with the - l channel in the middle of the scale commands to watch the progress as it occurs.

Presently, we have completely changed over to rendition 0.3 (node-js-scale-b). All clients will currently observe the variant 0.3 of the site. We have four imitations of rendition 0.3 and none of 0.2. In the event that you run a get rc command, you will see that despite everything we have a RC for 0.2 (node-js-scale-a). As a last cleanup, we can evacuate that controller totally, as pursues:

$ kubectl erase rc/node-js-scale-a

Application autoscaling

An ongoing element expansion to Kubernetes is that of the Horizontal Pod Autoscaler. This asset type is extremely valuable as it gives us an approach to naturally set edges for scaling our application. At present, that help is just for CPU, yet there is alpha help for custom application measurements too.

How about we utilize the node-js-scale Replication Controller from the earliest starting point of the part and include an autoscaling segment. Before we start, we should ensure we are downsized down to one copy utilizing the accompanying command:

$ kubectl scale - replicas=1 rc/node-js-scale

Presently we can create a Horizontal Pod Autoscaler with the accompanying hpa definition:

apiVersion: autoscaling/v1

kind: HorizontalPodAutoscaler

metadata:

name: node-js-scale

spec:

minReplicas: 1

maxReplicas: 3

scaleTargetRef:

apiVersion: v1

kind: ReplicationController

name: node-js-scale

targetCPUUtilizationPercentage: 20

Posting 4-6. node-js-scale-hpa.yaml

Feel free to create this with the kubectl create - f command. Presently we can list the hpas and get a portrayal too:

$ kubectl get hpa

We can likewise create autoscaling in the command line with the kubectl autoscale command. The first YAML will resemble the accompanying:

$kubectl autoscale rc/node-js-scale - min=1 - max=3 - cpu-percent=20

This will show us an autoscaler on the node-js-scale Replication Controller with a Target CPU of 30%. Also, you will see that the base units is set to 1 and most extreme is 3:

How about we likewise inquiry our cases to perceive what number of are running at this moment:

$ kubectl get cases - l name=node-js-scale

We should see just a single node-js-scale case on the grounds that our HPA is demonstrating 0% usage, so we should create some heap. We will utilize the well known blast application normal in numerous holder demos. The accompanying posting will assist us with making nonstop burden until we can hit the CPU limit for autoscaler:

apiVersion: v1

kind: ReplicationController

metadata:

name: boomload

spec:

copies: 1

selector:

application: loadgenerator

layout:

metadata:

names:

application: loadgenerator

spec:

compartments:

- image: williamyeh/blast

name: blast

command: ["/receptacle/sh","- c"]

args: ["while genuine ; do blast http://node-js-scale/ - c 10 - n 100 ; rest 1 ; done"]

Posting 4-7. boomload.yaml

Utilize the kubectl create - f command with this posting and then be prepared to begin checking the hpa. We can do this with the kubectl get hpa command we utilized before.

It might take a couple of seconds, yet we should begin to see the present CPU usage increment.

When it goes over the 20% limit we set the autoscaler will kick in:

When we see this, we can run kubectl get unit again and see there are presently a few node-

js-scale cases:

$ kubectl get cases - l name=node-js-scale

We can tidy up now by executing our heap age unit:

```
$ kubectl erase rc/boomload
```

Presently in the event that we watch the hpa, we should begin to see the CPU use drop. It might take a couple of moments, however, in the long run, we will return down to 0% CPU burden.

Scaling a bunch

Every one of these procedures are incredible for the scaling of the application, yet shouldn't something be said about the group itself. Sooner or later, you will pack the nodes full and need more assets to plan new units for your outstanding tasks at hand.

Autoscaling

At the point when you create your group, you can customize the beginning number of nodes (cronies) with the NUM_MINIONS condition variable. Of course, it is set to 4.

Moreover, the Kubernetes group has begun to incorporate autoscaling ability with the bunch itself. At present, this is the main help on GCE and GKE, however work is being done on different suppliers. This ability uses the KUBE_AUTOSCALER_MIN_NODES,

KUBE_AUTOSCALER_MAX_NODES,and
KUBE_ENABLE_CLUSTER_AUTOSCALER

condition

factors.

The accompanying model tells the best way to set the earth factors for autoscaling before running kube-up.sh:

$ send out NUM_MINIONS=5

$export KUBE_AUTOSCALER_MIN_NODES=2

$export KUBE_AUTOSCALER_MAX_NODES=5

$export KUBE_ENABLE_CLUSTER_AUTOSCALER=true

Additionally, remember that changing this after the bunch is begun will have no impact. You would need to tear down the group and create it by and by. Hence, this area will tell you the best way to add nodes to a current group without remaking it.

When you start a bunch with these settings, your group will consequently scale here and there with the base and most extreme points of confinement dependent on figure asset utilization in the group.

GKE groups likewise support autoscaling when propelled, when utilizing the alpha highlights. The first model will utilize a banner, for example, - empower autoscaling - min-nodes=2 - max-nodes=5 in a command-line dispatch.

Scaling up the group on GCE

In the event that you wish to scale out a current bunch, we can do it with a couple of steps. Physically scaling up your group on GCE is quite simple. The current pipes utilizes oversaw occasion bunches in GCE, which enable you to effectively include more machines of a standard arrangement to the gathering through a case format.

You can see this format effectively in the GCE comfort. To begin with, open the support; as a matter of course, this should open your default venture reassure. On the off chance that you are utilizing another venture for your Kubernetes group, essentially select it from the undertaking dropdown at the highest point of the page.

As an afterthought board, see under Compute and then Compute Engine, and select Instance formats. You should see a layout titled kubernetes-crony format. Note that the name could fluctuate marginally on the off chance that you've customized your group naming settings.

You'll see various settings, yet the meat of the format is under the Custom metadata. Here, you will see various condition factors and likewise a startup content that is pursued another machine case is created. These are the center segments that enable us to create new machines and have them naturally added to the accessible group nodes.

Since the layout for new machines is as of now created, it is extremely easy proportional out our bunch in GCE. Once in the Compute segment of the reassure, basically go to Instance bunches found right over the Instance layouts connect as an afterthought board. Once more, you should see a gathering titled kubernetes-crony gathering or something comparable.

You'll see a page with a CPU measurements chart and three cases recorded here. Naturally, the bunch creates three nodes. We can alter this gathering by tapping on the EDIT GROUP button at the highest point of the page:

You should see kubernetes-crony format chose in Instance layout that we checked on a minute back. You'll likewise observe an Autoscaling setting, which is Off as a matter of course and an example tally of 3. Basically, increase this to 4 and snap on Save. You'll be reclaimed to the gathering subtleties page and you'll see a spring up discourse indicating the pending changes.

You'll additionally observe some auto mending properties on the Instance Group alter page. This recreates bombed occurrences and enables you to set wellbeing checks just as an underlying postpone period before a move is made.

In no time flat, you'll have another case recorded on the subtleties page. We can test this is prepared utilizing the get nodes command from the command line:

$ kubectl get nodes

An expression of alert on autoscaling and scale down as a rule

To start with, on the off chance that we rehash the prior procedure and abatement the commencement to four, GCE will expel one node. In any case, it won't really be the node you just included. Fortunately cases will be rescheduled on the rest of the nodes. Be that as it may, it can just reschedule where assets are accessible. On the off chance that you are near full limit and shut down a node, there is a decent possibility that a few units won't have a spot to be rescheduled. What's more, this is certifiably not a live relocation, so any application state will be lost in the progress. Most importantly you ought to painstakingly think about the suggestions before downsizing or actualizing an autoscaling plan.

For more data on general autoscaling in GCE, allude to

the https://cloud.google.com/figure/docs/autoscaler/?hl=en_US#sc aling_based_on_cpu_utilization connect.

Scaling up the bunch on AWS

The AWS supplier code likewise makes it simple to scale up your bunch. Like GCE, the AWS arrangement utilizes autoscaling gatherings to create the default four flunky nodes. Later on, the autoscaling gatherings will ideally be coordinated into the Kubernetes bunch autoscaling usefulness. For the present, we will walk however a manual arrangement.

This can likewise be effectively adjusted utilizing the CLI or the web comfort. In the reassure, from the EC2 page, just go to the Auto Scaling Groups segment at the base of the menu on the left. You should see a name like kubernetes-flunky gathering

We can scale this gathering up effectively by tapping on Edit. At that point, change the Desired, Min, and Max esteems to 5 and snap on Save. In almost no time, you'll have the fifth node accessible. You can indeed check this utilizing the get nodes command.

Downsizing is a similar procedure, yet recall that we talked about similar contemplations in the past Scaling up the bunch on GCE area. Remaining tasks at hand could get abandoned or, at any rate, surprisingly restarted.

Scaling physically

For different suppliers, making new cronies may not be a computerized procedure. Contingent upon your supplier, you'll have to perform different manual advances. It tends to be useful to take a gander at the supplier explicit contents in the bunch catalog.

Summary

We should now be more OK with the essentials of use scaling in Kubernetes. We additionally took a gander at the inherent capacities so as to move refreshes just as a manual procedure for testing and gradually coordinating updates. We investigated how proportional the nodes of our basic group and increment the general limit with regards to our Kubernetes assets. At long last, we investigated a portion of the new auto scaling ideas for both the bunch and our applications themselves.

In the following part, we will take a gander at the most recent strategies for scaling and refreshing applications with the new arrangements asset type, just as a portion of different sorts of remaining tasks at hand we can run on Kubernetes.

5

Deployments, Jobs, and DaemonSets

This section will cover the different sorts of outstanding burdens that Kubernetes underpins. We will cover Deployments for applications that are normally refreshed and long running. We will likewise return to the points of use updates and steady rollouts utilizing Deployments. Also, we will see Jobs utilized for short-running undertakings. At long last, we will take a gander at DaemonSets, which enable projects to be run on each node in our Kubernetes bunch.

This section will talk about the accompanying:

Arrangements

Application scaling with arrangements

Application refreshes with arrangements

Jobs

DaemonSets

Organizations

In the past part, we investigated a portion of the center ideas for application refreshes utilizing the old moving update technique. Beginning with variant 1.2, Kubernetes included the Deployment build, which enhances the essential systems of moving update and Replication Controllers. As the name recommends, it gives us a better control of the code organization itself. Arrangements enable us to delay and resume application rollouts. Also, it keeps a background marked by past organizations and enables the client to effectively rollback to past variants.

In the accompanying, posting 5-1, we can see that the definition is fundamentally the same as a Replication Controller. The fundamental distinction is that we currently have a capacity to make changes and updates to the arrangement items and let Kubernetes oversee refreshing the hidden units and imitations for us:

apiVersion: augmentations/v1beta1

kind: Deployment

metadata:

name: node-js-convey

marks:

name: node-js-convey

spec:

reproductions: 1

format:

metadata:

marks:

name: node-js-convey

spec:

holders:

- name: node-js-convey

picture: jonbaier/case scaling:0.1 ports:

- containerPort: 80

Posting 5-1: node-js-deploy.yaml

We can run the comfortable create command with the discretionary - record banner so the making of the sending is recorded in the rollout history. Else, we will just observe resulting changes in the rollout history:

$ kubectl create - f node-js-deploy.yaml - record

You may need to include - validate=false if this beta kind isn't empowered on your bunch.

We should see a message about the organization being effectively created. After a couple of seconds, it will wrap up our unit, which we can check for ourselves with a get cases command. We add the - l banner to just observe the units applicable to this arrangement:

$ kubectl get units - l name=node-js-convey

We create an assistance similarly as we did with Replication Controllers. Coming up next is a Service definition for the arrangement we just created. We'll see that it is practically indistinguishable from the Services we created previously:

apiVersion: v1

kind: Service

metadata:

name: node-js-convey

marks:

name: node-js-convey

spec:

type: LoadBalancer

ports:

- port: 80 sessionAffinity: ClientIP selector:

name: node-js-convey

Posting 5-2. node-js-convey service.yaml

When this administration is created utilizing kubectl, you'll have the option to get to the sending cases through the administration IP or the administration name on the off chance that you are inside a unit on this namespace.

Scaling

The scale command works a similar route as it did in our Replication Controller. To scale up, we essentially utilize the organization name and indicate the new number of reproductions, as appeared here:

$ kubectl scale arrangement node-js-send - copies 3

In the event that all goes well, we'll essentially observe a message about the arrangement being scaled on the yield of our terminal window. We can check the quantity of running cases utilizing the get cases command from prior, again.

Updates and rollouts

Arrangements consider refreshing in a couple of different ways. To start with, there is the kubectl set command, which enables us to change the sending arrangement without redeploying physically. Right now, it takes into account refreshing the picture, however as new forms of our application or compartment picture are prepared, we should do this frequently.

We should investigate utilizing our organization from the past segment. We ought to have three reproductions running at the present time. Confirm this by running the get cases command with a channel for our arrangement:

$ kubectl get units - l name=node-js-send

Take one of the units recorded on our arrangement, supplant it in the accompanying command where it says {POD_NAME_FROM_YOUR_LISTING}, and run the command:

$ kubectl portray unit/{POD_NAME_FROM_YOUR_LISTING} | grep Image:

We should see a yield like the accompanying picture with the present picture form of 0.1:

Since we comprehend what our present sending is running, how about we attempt to refresh to the following form. This can be accomplished effectively utilizing the kubectl set command and indicating the new form, as appeared here:

$kubectl set picture sending/node-js-convey node-js-deploy=jonbaier/unit scaling:0.2

On the off chance that all goes well, we should see the content that says sending "node-js-convey" picture refreshed showed on the screen.

We can twofold check the status utilizing the accompanying rollout status command:

$ kubectl rollout status arrangement/node-js-send

We should see some content about the arrangement effectively turned out. In the event that you see any content about sitting tight for the rollout to complete, you may need to sit tight a minute for it to complete or on the other hand check the logs for issues.

When it's done, run the get units command as prior, again. This time we will see new units recorded:

By and by plug one of your case names into the depict command we ran before. This time we should see the picture has been refreshed to 0.2.

What occurred off camera is that Kubernetes has revealed another variant for us. It essentially creates another reproduction set with the new form. When this unit is on the web and sound it slaughters one of the more seasoned renditions. It proceeds with this conduct, scaling out the new form and downsizing the old renditions, until just the new cases are left.

It's important that the rollback definition enables us to control the case supplant strategy in our organization definition. There is a strategy.type field that defaults to RollingUpdate and the previous conduct. Alternatively, we can likewise determine Recreate as the substitution methodology and it will slaughter all the old units first before making the new forms.

History and rollbacks

One of the valuable highlights of the rollout programming interface is the capacity to follow the arrangement history. How about we do one more refresh before we check the history. Run the kubectl set command again and indicate adaptation 0.3:

$kubectl set picture arrangement/node-js-convey node-js-deploy=jonbaier/unit scaling:0.3

By and by we'll see message that says organization "node-js-send" picture refreshed showed on the screen. Presently run the get cases command again:

$ kubectl get units - l name=node-js-send

We should likewise investigate our arrangement history. Run the rollout history command:

$ kubectl rollout history sending/node-js-convey

As should be obvious, the history shows us the underlying organization creation, our first update to 0.2, and then our last update to 0.3. Notwithstanding status and history, the rollout command additionally underpins the delay, continue, and fix sub-commands. The rollout delay command enables us to stop a command while the rollout is still in progress. This can be valuable for investigating and likewise supportive for canary sort dispatches, where we wish to do last testing of the new form before turning out to the whole client base. At the point when we are prepared to proceed with the rollout, we can essentially utilize the rollout continue command.

Be that as it may, imagine a scenario in which something turns out badly. That is the place the rollout fix command and the rollout history itself is extremely handy. How about we recreate this by attempting to refresh to a variant of our unit that isn't yet accessible. We will set the picture to adaptation 42.0, which doesn't exist:

$kubectl set picture organization/node-js-convey node-js-deploy=jonbaier/ case scaling:42.0

We should at present observe the content that says sending "node-js-convey" picture refreshed

shown on the screen. However, on the off chance that we check the status, we will see that it is as yet pausing:

$ kubectl rollout status sending/node-js-convey

We can press Ctrl + C to murder the status command and then run the get units command again:

$ kubectl get cases - l name=node-js-convey

As we expected, it can't pull the 42.0 rendition of the picture since it doesn't exist. We may likewise have issues with arrangements in the event that we come up short on assets on the group or hit constrains that are set for our namespace. Furthermore, the organization can fizzle for various application-related causes, for example, wellbeing check disappointment, consent issues, and application bugs, obviously.

At whatever point an inability to rollout occurs, we can without much of a stretch rollback to a past rendition utilizing the rollout fix command. This command will return our organization to the past rendition:

$ kubectl rollout fix sending/node-js-convey

From that point forward, we can run a rollout status command again and we should see everything turned out effectively. Run the rollout history command again and we'll see both our endeavor to rollout form 42.0 and the return to 0.3:

We can likewise indicate the - to-modification banner when running a fix to rollback to a particular adaptation. This can be handy for times when our rollout succeeds, yet we find legitimate mistakes not far off.

Autoscaling

As should be obvious, Deployments are an extraordinary improvement over Replication Controllers enabling us to flawlessly refresh our applications, while incorporating with different assets of Kubernetes similarly.

Another region that we found in the past part, and additionally upheld for Deployments, is Horizontal Pod Autoscalers (HPAs). As you may have speculated, this likewise coordinates consummately with Deployments. We will stroll through a fast change of the HPAs from the past part, this time utilizing the Deployments we have created up until now:

apiVersion: autoscaling/v1

kind: HorizontalPodAutoscaler

metadata:

name: node-js-convey

spec:

minReplicas: 3

maxReplicas: 6

scaleTargetRef:

apiVersion: v1

kind: Deployment

name: node-js-convey

targetCPUUtilizationPercentage: 10

Posting 5-3. node-js-convey hpa.yaml

We have brought down the CPU edge to 10% and changed our base and greatest cases to 3 and 6, separately. Create the former HPA with our trusty kubectl create - f command. After this is finished, we can watch that it's accessible with the kubectl get hpa command:

We can likewise watch that we have just 3 cases running with the kubectl get convey command. Presently we should add some heap to trigger the autoscaler:

apiVersion: augmentations/v1beta1

kind: Deployment

metadata:

name: boomload-convey

spec:

reproductions: 1

format:

metadata:

marks:

application: loadgenerator-convey

spec:

holders:

- image: williamyeh/blast

name: blast convey

command: ["/container/sh","- c"]

args: ["while genuine ; do blast http://node-js-convey/ - c 10 - n 100 ; rest 1
;

done"]

Posting 5-4. boomload-deploy.yaml

Create posting 5-4 not surprisingly. Presently screen the HPA with the exchanging kubectl get

hpa and kubectl get send commands. After a couple of seconds, we should see the heap bounce above 10%. After a couple of more minutes, we ought to likewise observe the quantity of units increment as far as possible up to 6 imitations:

Once more, we can tidy this up by expelling our heap age case and holding up a couple of seconds:

$ kubectl erase convey boomload-send

Once more, on the off chance that we watch the HPA, we'll begin to see the CPU use drop. Following a couple of moments, we will return down to 0% CPU burden and then the Deployment will downsize to 3 reproductions.

Jobs

Organizations and Replication Controllers are an extraordinary method to guarantee long running applications are consistently up and ready to endure a wide exhibit of foundation disappointments. In any case, there are some utilization cases this doesn't address—explicitly short running, run once, errands just as routinely planned undertakings. In the two cases, we need the assignments to run until consummation, however then end and start again at the following booked interim.

To address this kind of outstanding task at hand, Kubernetes has included a Batch API, which incorporates the Job type. This sort will create 1 to n units and guarantee that they all rush to fulfillment with a fruitful exit. In light of restartPolicy, we can either enable cases to just come up short without retry (restartPolicy: Never) or retry when a units exits without fruitful finishing (restartPolicy: OnFailure). In this model, we will utilize the last strategy:

apiVersion: bunch/v1

kind: Job

metadata:

name: long-task

spec:

format:

metadata:

name: long-task

spec:

holders:

- name: long-task

picture: docker/whalesay

command: ["cowsay", "Completing that undertaking in a jiffy"]

restartPolicy: OnFailure

Posting 5-5: longtask.yaml

How about we feel free to run this with the accompanying command:

$ kubectl create - f longtask.yaml

On the off chance that all goes well, you'll see work "long-task" created imprinted on the screen.

This reveals to us the activity was created, yet doesn't let us know whether it finished effectively. To watch that, we have to inquiry the activity status with the accompanying command:

$ kubectl portray jobs/long-task

You should see that we had 1 errand that succeeded and in the Events logs, a SuccessfulCreate message. On the off chance that we use kubectl get cases command, we won't see our long-task cases in the rundown, yet we may see the message at the base if the posting states that there are finished jobs that are not appeared. We should run the command again with the - an or - show-all banner to see the long-task unit and the finished Job status.

How about we burrow somewhat more profound to demonstrate to ourselves the work was finished effectively. We could utilize the logs command to take a gander at the units logs. Be that as it may, we can likewise utilize the UI for this undertaking. Open a program and go to the accompanying UI URL: https://<your ace

ip>/ui/

Snap on Jobs and then long-task from the rundown, so we can see the subtleties. At that point, in the Pods area, click on the case recorded there.

This will give us the Pod subtleties page. At the base of the subtleties, click on View Logs and we will see the log yield

As should be obvious in the former picture, the whalesay holder is finished with the ASCII craftsmanship and our custom message from the runtime parameters in the model.

Different sorts of jobs

While this model gives an essential prologue to short running jobs, it just tends to the utilization instance of once and done errands. In actuality, bunch work is often done in Parallel or as a major aspect of a routinely happening assignment.

Parallel jobs

Utilizing Parallel jobs, we might be snatching assignments from a continuous line or just running a set number of errands that are not subject to one another. On account of jobs pulling from a line, our application must know about the conditions and have the rationale to choose how assignments are prepared and what to deal with straightaway. Kubernetes is essentially planning the jobs.

You can take in progressively about parallel jobs from the Kubernetes documentation and bunch API reference

Planned jobs

For assignments that need to run intermittently, Kubernetes has likewise discharged a CronJob type in alpha. As we may expect, this sort of occupation utilizes the hidden cron arranging to determine a calendar for the assignment we wish to run. Naturally, our bunch won't have the alpha group highlights empowered, however we can take a gander at a model CronJob inclining to figure out how these kinds of remaining tasks at hand will work going ahead:

apiVersion: group/v2alpha1

kind: CronJob

metadata:

name: long-task-cron

spec:

plan: "15 10 * 6"

jobTemplate:

spec:

layout:

spec:

compartments:

- name: long-task-cron

picture: docker/whalesay

command: ["cowsay", "Designers! Designers! Designers!

\n\n Saturday task

complete!"]

restartPolicy: OnFailure

Posting 5-6. longtask-cron.yaml

As should be obvious, the calendar partition mirrors a crontab with the accompanying organization: minute hour day-of month day-of-week

In this model, 15 10 * 6 creates an errand that will run each Saturday at 10:15 am.

DaemonSets

While Replication Controllers and Deployments are extraordinary at ensuring that a particular number of utilization occurrences are running, they do as such with regards to the best fit. This implies the scheduler searches for nodes that meet asset prerequisites (accessible CPU, specific stockpiling volumes, and so on) and attempts to spread across the nodes and zones.

This functions admirably for making profoundly accessible and shortcoming tolerant applications, however shouldn't something be said about situations where we need a specialist to run on each and every node in the group? While the default spread attempts to utilize different nodes, it doesn't ensure that each node will have a copy and, for sure, will just fill various nodes comparable to the amount determined in the RC or Deployment detail.

To facilitate this weight, Kubernetes presented DaemonSet, which basically characterizes a case to run on each and every node in the group or a characterized subset of those nodes. This can be valuable for various creation related exercises, for example, checking and logging specialists, security operators, and file system daemons.

Truth be told, Kubernetes as of now utilizes this ability for a portion of its center system parts. In the event that we review from Chapter 1, Introduction to Kubernetes, we saw a node-issue finder running on the nodes. This unit is really running on each node in the group

as DaemonSet. We can see this by questioning DaemonSets in the kube-system namespace:

$ kubectl get ds - namespace=kube-system

You can discover more data about node-issue locator just as yaml in the accompanying posting at:

etector:

apiVersion: augmentations/v1beta1

kind: DaemonSet

metadata:

name: node-issue locator v0.1

namespace: kube-system

marks:

k8s-application: node-issue locator

rendition: v0.1

kubernetes.io/bunch administration: "genuine"

spec:

format:

metadata:

marks:

k8s-application: node-issue locator

rendition: v0.1

kubernetes.io/bunch administration: "genuine"

spec:

hostNetwork: genuine

holders:

- name: node-issue locator

picture: gcr.io/google_containers/node-issue detector:v0.1
securityContext:

advantaged: genuine assets:

limits: cpu: "200m" memory: "100Mi"

demands: cpu: "20m" memory: "20Mi"

volumeMounts:

- name: log

mountPath:/log

readOnly: genuine

volumes:

- name: log hostPath:

way:/var/log/

Posting 5-7. node-issue indicator definition

Node choice

As referenced already, we can plan DaemonSets to run on a subset of nodes too. This can be accomplished utilizing something many refer to as nodeSelectors. These enable us to oblige the nodes a cases runs on, by searching for explicit marks and metadata. They just match key-esteem combines on the marks for every node. We can include our very own names or utilize those that are relegated as a matter of course.

We are not constrained to DaemonSets, as nodeSelectors really work with Pod definitions also and are not restricted to DaemonSets. We should investigate work model (a slight alteration of our previous long-task model).

To begin with, we can see these on the nodes themselves. We should get the names of our nodes:

$ kubectl get nodes

Utilize a name from the yield of the past command and attachment it into this one:

$ kubectl portray node <node-name>

We should now add an epithet name to this node:

$ kubectl mark nodes <node-name> nodenickname=trusty-steve

On the off chance that we run the kubectl depict node command once more, we will see this mark recorded alongside the defaults. Presently we can plan remaining tasks at hand and determine this particular node. Here is an adjustment of our prior long-running assignment with nodeSelector included:

apiVersion: group/v1

kind: Job

metadata:

name: long-task-ns

spec:

layout:

metadata:

name: long-task-ns

spec:

compartments:

- name: long-task-ns

picture: docker/whalesay

command: ["cowsay", "Completing that assignment in a jiffy"] restartPolicy: OnFailure

nodeSelector:

nodenickname: trusty-steve

Posting 5-8. longtask-nodeselector.yaml

Create the activity from this posting with kubectl create - f.

When that succeeds, it will create a case dependent on the former determination. Since we have characterized nodeSelector, it will attempt to run the unit on nodes that have coordinating marks and fizzle on the off chance that it finds no candidates. We can discover the unit by determining the activity name in our question, as pursues:

$ kubectl get units - a - l work name=long-task-ns

We utilize the - a banner to show all cases. Jobs are fleeting and once they enter the finished state, they won't appear in an essential kubectl get pods question. We additionally utilize the - l banner to determine units with the activity name=long-task-ns mark. This will give us the unit name which we can push into the accompanying command:

$ kubectl depict unit <Pod-Name-For-Job> | grep Node:

The outcome should show the name of the node this unit was run on. On the off chance that all has gone well, it should coordinate the node we named a couple of steps prior with the trusty-steve name.

Summary

Presently you ought to have a decent establishment of the center builds in Kubernetes. We investigated the new Deployment reflection and how it enhances the essential Replication Controller, taking into consideration smooth updates and strong coordination with administrations and autoscaling. We likewise took a gander at different sorts of remaining task at hand in jobs and DaemonSets. You figured out how to run short-running or bunch assignments just as how to run specialists on each node in our group. At last, we investigated node determination and how that can be utilized to channel the nodes in the bunch utilized for our remaining tasks at hand.

We will expand on what you realized in this section and take a gander at the Stateful applications in the following part, investigating both basic application segments and the information itself.

6

Storage and Running Stateful Applications

In this section, we will talk about how to connect persevering volumes and create stockpiling for stateful applications and information. We will stroll through capacity concerns and how we can continue information across units and the holder life cycle. We will investigate the PersistentVolumes types just as PersistentVolumeClaim. At long last, we will investigate the new StatefulSets discharge in adaptation 1.5.

This part will examine the accompanying points:

Relentless stockpiling

PersistentVolumes

PersistentVolumeClaims

StorageClasses

StatefulSets

174

Persevering stockpiling

Up until now, we just worked with outstanding tasks at hand that we could begin and stop freely, with no issue. In any case, true applications often convey state and record information that we like (even demand) not to lose. The transient idea of holders themselves can be a major test. In the event that you review our talk of layered file systems in Chapter 1, Introduction to Kubernetes, the top layer is writable. (It's additionally icing, which is delightful.) However, when the holder kicks the bucket, the information goes with it. The equivalent is valid for slammed holders that Kubernetes restarts.

This is the place volumes or circles become an integral factor. A volume that exists outside the compartment enables us to spare our significant information across holders blackouts. Further, in the event that we have a volume at the unit level, information can be shared between compartments in a similar application stack and inside a similar case.

Docker itself has some help for volumes, however Kubernetes gives us tireless stockpiling that keeps going past the lifetime of a solitary holder. The volumes are attached to units and live amazing those cases. Also, a case can have different volumes from an assortment of sources. We should investigate a portion of these sources.

Transitory plates

Perhaps the most straightforward approaches to accomplish improved ingenuity in the midst of compartment accidents and information sharing inside a case is to utilize the emptydir volume. This volume type can be utilized with either the capacity volumes of the node machine itself or a discretionary RAM plate for better.

Once more, we improve our tirelessness past a solitary holder, yet when a case is evacuated, the information will be lost. Machine reboot will likewise clear any information from RAM-type plates. There might be times when we simply need some common transitory space or have holders that procedure information and hand it off to another compartment before they kick the bucket. Whatever the case, here is a speedy case of utilizing this brief plate with the RAM-upheld alternative.

Open your preferred proofreader and create a file like the one in the accompanying Listing 6-1:

apiVersion: v1

kind: Pod

metadata:

name: memory-pd

spec:

holders:

- image: nginx:latest ports:

- containerPort: 80 name: memory-pd volumeMounts:

- mountPath:/memory-pd

name: memory-volume

volumes:

- name: memory-volume emptyDir:

medium: Memory

Posting 6-1: stockpiling memory.yaml

The previous model is most likely of natural at this point, however we will by and by issue a create command pursued by an executive command to see the envelopes in the holder:

$ kubectl create - f stockpiling memory.yaml

$ kubectl executive memory-pd - ls - lh | grep memory-pd

This will give us a slam shell in the holder itself. The ls command shows us a memory-pd organizer at the top level. We use grep to channel the yield, yet you can run the command without | grep memory-pd to see all organizers:

Once more, this envelope is very brief as everything is put away in the node's (minion's) RAM. At the point when the node gets restarted, every one of the files will be deleted. We will take a gander at an increasingly changeless model straightaway.

Cloud volumes

Numerous organizations will as of now have critical foundation running in general society cloud. Fortunately, Kubernetes has local help for the sturdy stockpiling gave by two of the most well known suppliers.

GCE steady plates

We have the accompanying from the GCE site:

Google Persistent Disk is solid and elite square stockpiling for the Google Cloud Platform. Persevering Disk give SSD and HDD stockpiling which can be connected to cases running in either Google Compute Engine or Google Container Engine.

Capacity volumes can be straightforwardly resized, immediately upheld up, and offer the capacity to help synchronous perusers. (you can allude to more insights regarding this in point 1 in the References segment toward the finish of the section)

How about we create another GCE constant circle.

1.From the comfort, in Compute Engine, go to Disks. On this new screen, click on the Create Disk button. We'll be given a screen like the accompanying GCE new constant circle picture.

2.Choose a name for this volume and give it a concise depiction. Ensure that Zone is equivalent to the nodes in your group. GCE PDs must be appended to machines in a similar zone.

3.Enter mysite-volume-1 in the Name field. Pick the zone coordinating in any event one node in your bunch. Pick None (clear circle) for Source type and give 10

(10 GB) as incentive in Size (GB). At long last, click on Create:

The decent thing about PDs on GCE is that they consider mounting to different machines (nodes for our situation). Be that as it may, when mounting to various machines, the volume must be in perused just mode. Along these lines, allows first mount this to a solitary case, so we can create a few files. Use Listing 6-2: stockpiling gce.yaml as pursues to create a unit that will mount the plate in read/compose mode:

apiVersion: v1

kind: Pod

metadata:

name: test-gce

spec:

holders:

- image: nginx:latest ports:

- containerPort: 80 name: test-gce volumeMounts:

- mountPath:/usr/share/nginx/html

name: gce-pd

volumes:

- name: gce-pd gcePersistentDisk:

pdName: mysite-volume-1

fsType: ext4

Posting 6-2: stockpiling gce.yaml

Initially, how about we issue a create command pursued by a depict command to discover which node it is running on:

$kubectl create - f stockpiling gce.yaml

$kubectl depict case/test-gce

Note the node and spare the case IP address for some other time. At that point, open a SSH session into that node:

$gcloud process - venture "<Your venture ID>" ssh - zone "<your gce zone>" "<Node running test-gce pod>"

Since we've just taken a gander at the volume from inside the running holder, how about we get to it legitimately from the node (follower) itself this time. We will run a df command to see where it is mounted, yet we should change to root first:

$ sudo su -

$ df - h | grep mysite-volume-1

As should be obvious, the GCE volume is mounted legitimately to the node itself. We can utilize the mount way recorded in the yield of the prior df command. Use album to change to the envelope now. At that point, create another file named index.html with your preferred supervisor:

$cd/var/lib/kubelet/modules/kubernetes.io/gce-pd/mounts/ mysite-volume-1

$vi index.html

Enter a curious message, for example, Hello from my GCE PD!. Presently spare the file and leave the manager. In the event that you review from Listing 6-2, the PD is mounted straightforwardly to the Nginx HTML catalog. In this way, we should test this out while regardless we have the SSH session open on the node. Do a basic twist command to the unit IP we recorded before:

$ twist <Pod IP from Describe>

You should see Hello from my GCE PD! or on the other hand whatever message you spared in the index.html file. In a certifiable situation, we can utilize the volume for a whole site or some other focal stockpiling. How about we investigate running a lot of burden adjusted web servers all indicating a similar volume.

Initially, leave the SSH session with two leave commands. Before we continue, we should evacuate our test-gce unit with the goal that the volume can be mounted perused uniquely across various nodes:

$ kubectl erase case/test-gce

Presently we can create a RC that will run three web servers all mounting the equivalent persevering plate, as pursues:

apiVersion: v1

kind: ReplicationController

metadata:

name: http-pd

marks:

name: http-pd

spec:

imitations: 3

selector:

name: http-pd

format:

metadata:

name: http-pd

marks:

name: http-pd

spec:

holders:

- picture: nginx:latest

ports:

- containerPort: 80 name: http-pd volumeMounts:

- mountPath:/usr/share/nginx/html

name: gce-pd

volumes:

- name: gce-pd gcePersistentDisk:

pdName: mysite-volume-1

fsType: ext4

readOnly: genuine

Posting 6-3: http-pd-controller.yaml

How about we likewise create an outer help, so we can see it from outside the bunch:

apiVersion: v1

kind: Service

metadata:

name: http-pd

names:

name: http-pd

spec:

type: LoadBalancer

ports:

- name: http

convention: TCP

port: 80

selector:

name: http-pd

Posting 6-4: http-pd-service.yaml

Feel free to create these two assets now. Trust that the outside IP will get relegated. After this, a portray command will give us the IP we can use in a program:

$ kubectl depict administration/http-pd

On the off chance that you don't see the LoadBalancer Ingress field yet, it likely needs more opportunity to get allocated. Type the IP address from LoadBalancer Ingress into a program, and you should see your natural index.html file appear with the content we entered beforehand!

AWS Elastic Block Store

K8s likewise underpins AWS Elastic Block Store (EBS) volumes. Like the GCE PDs, EBS volumes are required to be joined to an example running in a similar accessibility zone. A further restriction is that EBS must be mounted to a solitary example at once.

For quickness, we won't stroll through an AWS model, yet an example YAML file is incorporated to kick you off. Once more, make sure to create the EBS volume before your case:

apiVersion: v1

kind: Pod

metadata:

name: test-aws

spec:

compartments:

- image: nginx:latest ports:

- containerPort: 80 name: test-aws volumeMounts:

- mountPath:/usr/share/nginx/html

name: aws-pd

volumes:

- name: aws-pd awsElasticBlockStore:

volumeID: aws://<availability-zone>/<volume-id>

fsType: ext4

Posting 6-5: stockpiling aws.yaml

Other stockpiling alternatives

Kubernetes underpins an assortment of different kinds of capacity volumes. A full rundown can be found here:

Here are a not many that might be exceptionally compelling:

nfs: This sort enables us to mount a Network File Share (NFS), which can be valuable for both enduring the information and sharing it across the foundation

gitrepo: As you may have speculated, this alternative clones a Git repo into another and void organizer

PersistentVolumes and StorageClasses

So far, we've seen instances of legitimately provisioning the capacity inside our unit definitions. This works very well in the event that you have full power over your group and foundation, yet at bigger scales, application proprietors will need to utilize capacity that is overseen independently. Commonly, a focal IT group or the cloud supplier itself will deal with the subtleties behind provisioning stockpiling and leave the application proprietors to stress over their essential concern, the application itself.

So as to suit this, we need some route for the application to determine and demand stockpiling without being worried about how that capacity is given. This is the place

PersistentVolumes and PersistentVolumeClaims come into play. PersistentVolumes are like volumes we created before, yet they are given by the bunch regulate and are not reliant on a specific case. This volume would then be able to be guaranteed by units utilizing PersistentVolumeClaims.

PersistentVolumeClaims enables us to indicate the subtleties of the capacity required. We can characterized the measure of capacity just as the entrance type, for example, ReadWriteOnce (peruse and compose by one node), ReadOnlyMany (read-just by numerous nodes), and ReadWriteMany (peruse and compose by numerous nodes). Obviously, which modes are bolstered is subject to the support stockpiling supplier. For instance, we found in the AWS EBS model that mounting to different nodes was impossible.

Furthermore, Kubernetes gives two different techniques to indicating certain groupings or sorts of capacity volumes. The first is the utilization of selectors as we have seen beforehand for case determination. Here, names can be applied to capacity volumes and then claims can reference these names to additionally channel the volume they are given. Second, Kubernetes has an idea of StorageClass which permits us determine a capacity provisioner and parameters for the sort of volumes it arrangements.

We will plunge into StorageClasses in the following segment, yet here is a speedy case of a PersistentVolumeClaims for delineation purposes. You can find in the comments that we demand 1Gi of capacity in ReadWriteOnce mode with a StorageClass of solidstate and mark of aws-stockpiling.

kind: PersistentVolumeClaim

apiVersion: v1

metadata:

name: demo-guarantee

explanations:

volume.beta.kubernetes.io/capacity class: "solidstate"

spec:

accessModes:

- ReadWriteOnce assets:

demands: stockpiling: 1Gi

selector:

matchLabels:

discharge: "aws-capacity"

Posting 6-6: pvc-example.yaml

StatefulSets

The reason for StatefulSets is to give some consistency and consistency to application organizations with stateful information. Up to this point, we have sent applications to the bunch characterizing free prerequisites around required assets, for example, PC and capacity. The group has booked our remaining task at hand on any node that can meet these prerequisites. While we can utilize a portion of these imperatives to send in a progressively unsurprising way, it will be useful on the off chance that we had a develop worked to assist us with giving this consistency.

StatefulSets were set to GA in 1.6 as we went to press. There were beforehand beta in rendition 1.5 and were known as PetSets preceding that (alpha in 1.3 and 1.4).

This is the place StatefulSets come in. StatefulSets furnish us first with numbered and dependable naming for both system access and capacity claims. The cases themselves are names with the accompanying show, where N is from 0 to the quantity of copies:

"Name of Set"- N

This implies a Statefulset called db with 3 reproductions will create the accompanying units:

db-0

db-1

db-2

This gives Kubernetes an approach to relate arrange names and PersistentVolumes with explicit cases. Moreover, it additionally serves to arrange creation and end of units. Unit will be begun from 0 to N and ended from N to 0.

A stateful model

We should investigate a case of a stateful application. To begin with, we will need to create and utilize a StorageClass as we talked about before. This will enable us to guide into the Google Cloud Persistent Disk provisioner. The Kubernetes people group is building provisioners for an assortment of StorageClasses including GCP and AWS. Every provisioner has its own arrangement of parameters accessible. Both GCP and AWS suppliers let you pick the kind of plate (strong state, standard, and so on) just as the flaw zone which is expected to coordinate the unit appending to it. AWS moreover enables you to determine encryption parameters just as IOPs for Provisioned IOPs volumes. There are various different provisioners underway including Azure and an assortment of non-cloud choices:

kind: StorageClass

apiVersion: storage.k8s.io/v1beta1

metadata:

name: solidstate

provisioner: kubernetes.io/gce-pd

parameters:

type: pd-ssd

zone: us-central1-b

Posting 6-7: solidstate-sc.yaml

Utilize the accompanying command with the former inclining to create a StorageClass sort of

SSD drives in us-central1-b:

$ kubectl create - f solidstate.yaml

Next, we will create a StatefulSet kind with our trusty httpwhalesay demo (you can allude to more insights regarding this in point 2 in the References segment toward the finish of the part). While this application includes any genuine state, we can see the capacity asserts and investigate the correspondence way:

apiVersion: applications/v1beta1

kind: StatefulSet

metadata:

name: whaleset

spec:

serviceName: sayhey-svc

reproductions: 3

layout:

metadata:

names:

application: sayhey

spec:

terminationGracePeriodSeconds: 10

compartments:

- name: sayhey

picture: jonbaier/httpwhalesay:0.2

command: ["node", "index.js", "Whale it up!."]

ports:

- containerPort: 80

name: web

volumeMounts:

- name: www

mountPath:/usr/share/nginx/html

volumeClaimTemplates:

- metadata:

name: www

comments:

volume.beta.kubernetes.io/capacity class: solidstate spec:

accessModes: ["ReadWriteOnce"]

assets:

demands:

capacity: 1Gi

Posting 6-8: sayhey-statefulset.yaml

Utilize the accompanying command to get the opportunity to begin the production of this StatefulSet. In the event that you watch case creation intently, you will see it create whaleset-0, whaleset-1, and whaleset-2 in progression:

$ kubectl create - f sayhey-statefulset.yaml

Following this, we can see our StatefulSet and the comparing units utilizing the well-known get subcommand:

$kubectl get statefulsets

$kubectl get units

Contingent upon your planning, the units may in any case be making. As should be obvious in the former picture, the third holder is as yet being spun up.

We can likewise observe the volumes the set has created and guarantee for each case. First PersistentVolumes themselves:

$ kubectl get pv

The first command should show the three PersistentVolumes named www-whaleset-N. We see the size is 1Gi and the entrance mode is set to ReadWriteOnce (RWO) similarly as we characterized in our StorageClass:

You'll see a great part of similar settings here likewise with the PVs themselves. You may likewise see the finish of the case name (or PV name in the past posting) looks like www-whaleset-N. www is the mount name we determined in the previous YAML definition. This is then affixed to the case name to create the real PV and PVC name. One more territory we can guarantee that the best possible circle is connected with it is coordinating case.

Another zone where this arrangement is significant is in the system correspondence. StatefulSets additionally give reliable naming here. Before we can do this, we should create a help endpoint so we have a typical passage point for approaching solicitations:

apiVersion: v1

kind: Service

metadata:

name: sayhey-svc

names:

application: sayhey

spec:

ports:

- port: 80

name: web

clusterIP: None

selector:

application: sayhey

Posting 6-9: sayhey-svc.yaml

$ kubectl create - f sayhey-svc.yaml

Presently we should open a shell in one of the cases and check whether we can speak with another in the set:

$ kubectl executive whaleset-0 - I - t slam

The former command gives us a slam shell in the first whaleset unit. We would now be able to utilize the Service name to make a basic HTTP demand. We can utilize both the short name, sayhey-

svc, and the completely qualified name, sayhey-svc.default.svc.cluster.local:

$ twist sayhey-svc

$ twist sayhey-svc.default.svc.cluster.local

You'll see a yield like the accompanying picture. The administration endpoint goes about as a typical correspondence point for every one of the three cases:

Presently we should check whether we can speak with a particular pod in the StatefulSet. As we saw before, the StatefulSet named the case in a methodical way. It additionally gives them hostnames along these lines so that there is a particular DNS passage for each unit in the set. Once more, we will see the show of "Name of Set"- N and then include the completely qualified assistance URL. The accompanying model shows this for whaleset-1, which is the second Pod in our set:

$ twist whaleset-1.sayhey-svc.default.svc.cluster.local

Running this command from our current Bash shell in whaleset-0 will show us the yield from whaleset-1:

You can exit out of this shell now with exit.

For learning purposes, it can likewise be informative to depict a portion of the things from this area in more detail. For instance, kubectl portray svc sayhey-svc will give all of us three case IP address in the administration endpoints.

Summary

In this section, we investigated an assortment of constant stockpiling alternatives and how to execute them with our units. We took a gander at PersistentVolumes and likewise PersistentVolumeClaims, which enable us to isolate capacity provisioning and application stockpiling demands.

Furthermore, we took a gander at StorageClasses for provisioning gatherings of capacity as indicated by a detail.

We additionally investigated the new StatefulSets reflection and figured out how we can send stateful applications in a steady and requested way. In the following section, we will see how to coordinate Kubernetes with Continuous Integration and Delivery pipelines.

Continuous Delivery

This part will tell the peruser the best way to coordinate their assemble pipeline and organizations with a Kubernetes bunch. It will cover the idea of utilizing Gulp.js and Jenkins related to your Kubernetes group.

This part will examine the accompanying themes:

Coordinating with nonstop organization pipeline

Utilizing Gulp.js with Kubernetes

Coordinating Jenkins with Kubernetes

Coordinating with nonstop conveyance pipeline

Persistent reconciliation and conveyance are key segments to present day improvement shops. Speed to market or interim to-income are urgent for any organization that is making their very own software. We'll perceive how Kubernetes can support you.

CI/CD (short for Continuous Integration/Continuous Delivery) often requires vaporous form and test servers to be accessible at whatever point changes are pushed to the code archive. Docker and Kubernetes are appropriate for this assignment, as it's anything but difficult to create compartments in no time flat and similarly as simple to expel them after forms are run. What's more, in the event that you as of now have a huge segment of foundation accessible on your bunch, it can bode well to use the inactive limit with respect to fabricates and testing.

In this article, we will investigate two prevalent instruments utilized in building and conveying software:

Gulp.js: This is a straightforward errand sprinter used to mechanize the fabricate procedure utilizing JavaScript and Node.js

Jenkins: This is a completely fledged nonstop joining server

Gulp.js

Gulp.js gives us the system to do Build as code. Like Infrastructure as code, this enables us to automatically characterize our construct procedure. We will stroll through a short guide to exhibit how you can create a total work process from a Docker picture work to the last Kubernetes administration.

Essentials

For this segment of the article, you will require a NodeJS domain introduced and prepared including the node bundle chief (npm). In the event that you don't as of now have these bundles introduced, you can discover directions for introducing them at

https://docs.npmjs.com/beginning/introducing node.

You can check whether NodeJS is introduced accurately with a node - v command.

You'll additionally require Docker CE and a DockerHub record to push another picture. You can discover guidelines to introduce Docker CE at https://docs.docker.com/establishment/.

You can without much of a stretch create a DockerHub account at https://hub.docker.com/.

After you have your qualifications, you can sign in with the CLI utilizing $ docker login command.

Swallow manufacture model

How about we start by making a venture catalog named node-swallow:

$mkdir node-swallow

$cd node-swallow

Next, we will introduce the swallow bundle and check whether it's prepared by running the npm command with the variant banner, as pursues:

$ npm introduce - g swallow

You may need to open another terminal window to ensure that swallow is on your way.

Likewise, try to explore back to your node-swallow catalog:

$ swallow - v

Next, we will introduce swallow locally in our venture envelope just as the swallow git and swallow shell modules, as pursues:

$npm introduce - spare dev swallow

$npm introduce swallow git - spare

$npm introduce - spare dev swallow shell

At long last, we have to create a Kubernetes controller and administration definition file, just as a gulpfile.js file, to run every one of our assignments. Once more, these files are accessible in the book file group, in the event that you wish to duplicate them. Allude to the accompanying code:

apiVersion: v1

kind: ReplicationController

metadata:

name: node-swallow

names:

name: node-swallow

spec:

reproductions: 1

selector:

name: node-swallow

layout:

metadata:

names:

name: node-swallow

spec:

compartments:

- name: node-swallow

picture: <your username>/node-gulp:latest

imagePullPolicy: Always ports:

- containerPort: 80

Posting 7-1: node-swallow controller.yaml

As should be obvious, we have an essential controller. You should supplant <your username>/node-gulp:latest with your Docker Hub username:

apiVersion: v1

kind: Service

metadata:

name: node-swallow

names:

name: node-swallow

spec:

type: LoadBalancer

ports:

- name: http

convention: TCP

port: 80

selector:

name: node-swallow

Posting 7-2: node-swallow service.yaml

Next, we have a basic help that chooses the units from our controller and creates an outside burden balancer for access, as prior:

var swallow = require('gulp');

var git = require('gulp-git');

var shell = require('gulp-shell');

/Clone a remote repo gulp.task('clone', function(){

return   git.clone('https://github.com/jonbaierCTP/beginning with-kubernetes-s e.git', work (fail) {

in the event that (fail) toss blunder; });

});

/Update codebase gulp.task('pull', function(){

return git.pull('origin', 'ace', {cwd: './beginning with-kubernetes-se'}, work
(fail) {

in the event that (fail) toss blunder; });

});

/Build Docker Image

gulp.task('docker-construct', shell.task([

'docker construct - t <your username>/node-swallow ./beginning with-

kubernetes-se/docker-picture source/compartment data/', 'docker push
<your username>/node-swallow'

]));

/Run New Pod

gulp.task('create-kube-unit', shell.task([

'kubectl create - f node-swallow controller.yaml', 'kubectl create - f
node-swallow service.yaml'

]));

/Update Pod

gulp.task('update-kube-unit', shell.task([

'kubectl erase - f node-swallow controller.yaml', 'kubectl create - f
node-swallow controller.yaml'

]));

Posting 7-3: gulpfile.js

At last, we have the gulpfile.js file. This is the place all our manufacture undertakings are characterized. Once more, fill in your Docker Hub username in both the <your username>/node-swallow segments.

Glancing through the file, first, the clone task downloads our picture source code from GitHub. The force undertakings execute a git pull on the cloned archive. Next, the docker-manufacture command fabricates a picture from the holder data subfolder and drives it to DockerHub. At long last, we have the create-kube-unit and update-kube-case commands. As you can figure, the create-kube-unit command creates our controller and administration just because, while the update-kube-case command essentially replaces the controller.

How about we feel free to run these commands and see our start to finish work process:

$ swallow clone

$ swallow docker-manufacture

The first run through, you can run the create-kube-unit command, as pursues:

$ swallow create-kube-unit

This is the long and short of it. In the event that we run a snappy kubectl portray command for the node-swallow administration, we can get the outside IP for our new assistance. Peruse to that IP and you'll see the well-known compartment information application running. Note that the host begins with node-swallow, similarly as we named it in the recently referenced case definition:

On consequent updates, run the force and refresh kube-case commands, as appeared here:

$ swallow pull

$ swallow docker-construct

$ swallow update-kube-unit

This is an exceptionally basic model, however you can start to perceive that it is so natural to arrange your fabricate and sending start to finish with a couple of straightforward lines of code. Next, we will see how to utilize Kubernetes to really run assembles utilizing Jenkins.

Kubernetes module for Jenkins

One way we can utilize Kubernetes for our CI/CD pipeline is to run our Jenkins fabricate slaves in a containerized situation. Fortunately, there is as of now a module, composed via Carlos Sanchez, which enables you to run Jenkins slaves in Kubernetes' units.

Requirements

You'll require a Jenkins server handy for this next model. On the off chance that you don't have one you can use, there is a Docker picture accessible at https://hub.docker.com/_/jenkins/.

Running it from the Docker CLI is as straightforward as this:

docker run - name myjenkins - p 8080:8080 - v/var/jenkins_home Jenkins

Introducing modules

Sign in to your Jenkins server, and from your home dashboard, click on Manage Jenkins.

At that point, select Manage Plugins from the rundown.

A note for those introducing another Jenkins server: When you first sign in to the Jenkins server, it requests that you introduce modules. Pick the default ones or no modules will be introduced:

The certifications module is required, however ought to be introduced of course. We can check the

Introduced tab if all else fails

Next, we can tap on the Available tab. The Kubernetes module ought to be situated under Cluster Management and Distributed Build or Misc (cloud). There are numerous modules, so you can on the other hand scan for Kubernetes on the page. Check the case for Kubernetes Plugin and snap on Install without restart.

In the event that you wish to introduce a nonstandard form or simply prefer to tinker, you can alternatively download the modules. The most recent Kubernetes and Durable Task modules can be found here:

Kubernetes module:

https://wiki.jenkins-ci.org/show/JENKINS/Kubernetes+Plugin

Tough Task module:

https://wiki.jenkins-ci.org/show/JENKINS/Durable+Task+Plugin

Next, we can tap on the Advanced tab and look down to Upload Plugin. Explore to the tough task.hpi file and tap on Upload. You should see a screen that shows an introducing progress bar. Following a moment or two, it will refresh to Success.

At last, introduce the principle Kubernetes module. On the left-hand side, click on Manage Plugins and then the Advanced tab by and by. This time, transfer the kubernetes.hpi file and tap on Upload. Following a couple of moments, the establishment ought to be finished.

Designing the Kubernetes module

Snap on Back to Dashboard or the Jenkins connect in the upper left corner. From the primary dashboard page, click on the Credentials connect. Pick a space from the rundown; for my situation, I simply utilized the default Global certifications area. Snap on Add Credentials:

Leave Kind as Username with secret phrase and Scope as Global. Include your Kubernetes administrator certifications. Recall that you can discover these by running the config command:

$ kubectl config see

You can leave ID clear, give it a reasonable portrayal, and snap on the OK button.

Since we have our accreditations spared, we can include our Kubernetes server. Snap on the Jenkins connect in the upper left corner and then Manage Jenkins. From that point, select Configure System and look over right down to the Cloud area. Select Kubernetes from the Add another cloud dropdown and a Kubernetes area will show up

You'll have to determine the URL for your lord as https://<Master IP>/.

Next, pick the certifications we included starting from the drop list. Since Kubernetes utilize a self-marked testament of course, you'll likewise need to check the Disable https authentication check checkbox.

Snap on Test Connection and if all goes well, you should see Connection effective showing up by the catch.

In the event that you are utilizing a more established form of the module, you may not see the Disable https authentication check checkbox. If so, you should introduce oneself marked declaration straightforwardly on the Jenkins Master.

At long last, we will include a case format by picking Kubernetes Pod Template from the Add Pod Template dropdown alongside Images.

This will create another new area. Use jenkins-slave for the Name and Labels area. Snap on Add by Containers and again use jenkins-slave for the Name. Use

csanchez/jenkins-slave for the Docker Image and leave/home/jenkins for the

Working Directory.

Marks can be utilized later on in the assemble settings to constrain the work to utilize the Kubernetes bunch:

Snap on Save and you are good to go. Presently, new forms created in Jenkins can utilize the slaves in the Kubernetes case we just created.

Here is another note about firewalls. The Jenkins Master should be reachable by every one of the machines in your Kubernetes bunch, as the case could land anyplace. You can discover your port settings in Jenkins under Manage Jenkins and Configure Global Security.

Reward fun

Fabric8 charges itself as a joining stage. It incorporates an assortment of logging, observing, and ceaseless conveyance apparatuses. It additionally has a decent reassure, an API vault, and a 3D game that gives you a chance to take shots at your units. It's an extremely cool task, and it really runs on Kubernetes. Allude to http://fabric8.io/.

It's a simple single command to set up on your Kubernetes group, so allude to http://fabric8.io/direct/getStarted/gke.html.

Summary

We took a gander at two persistent mix devices that can be utilized with Kubernetes. We did a concise stroll through of conveying the Gulp.js task on our group. We additionally took a gander at another module used to coordinate Jenkins incorporate slaves with your Kubernetes bunch. You should now have a superior feeling of how Kubernetes can incorporate with your own CI/CD pipeline.

Monitoring and Logging

This section will cover the use and customization of both implicit and outsider monitoring apparatuses on our Kubernetes group. We will cover how to utilize the apparatuses to screen the wellbeing and execution of our group. Furthermore, we will take a gander at worked in logging, the Google Cloud Logging administration, and Sysdig.

This section will talk about the following themes:

How Kuberentes utilizes cAdvisor, Heapster, InfluxDB, and Grafana

Customizing the default Grafana dashboard

Using FluentD and Grafana

Installing and using logging apparatuses

Working with well known outsider devices, for example, StackDriver and Sysdig, to expand our monitoring abilities

Monitoring activities

True monitoring goes a long ways past checking whether a system is ready for action. Despite the fact that wellbeing checks, similar to those you learned in Chapter 2, Pods, Services, Replication Controllers, and Labels, in the Health checks segment, can assist us with isolating issue applications. Activity groups can best serve the business when they can envision the issues and relieve them before a system goes offline.

Best practices in monitoring are to gauge the exhibition and use of center assets and watch for patterns that stray from the ordinary baseline. Containers are not different here, and a key part to managing our Kubernetes group is having a reasonable view into execution and accessibility of the OS, arrange, system (CPU and memory), and capacity assets over all hubs.

In this part, we will examine a few choices to screen and quantify the presentation and accessibility of all our group assets. What's more, we will take a gander at a couple of choices for alerting and warnings when unpredictable patterns begin to develop.

Worked in monitoring

On the off chance that you review from Chapter 1, Introduction to Kubernetes, we noticed that our hubs were at that point running various monitoring administrations. We can see these indeed by running the get units command with the kube-system namespace determined as pursues:

$ kubectl get units - namespace=kube-system

Again, we see an assortment of administrations, yet how does this all fit together? In the event that you review the Node (some time ago minions) segment from Chapter 2, Pods, Services, Replication Controllers, and Labels, every hub is running a kublet. The kublet is the main interface for hubs to interact and refresh the API server. One such update is the measurements of the hub assets. The genuine reporting of the asset utilization is performed by a program named cAdvisor.

cAdvisor is another open-source venture from Google, which gives different measurements on container asset use. Measurements include CPU, memory, and system insights. There is no compelling reason to enlighten cAdvisor regarding individual containers; it gathers the measurements for all containers on a hub and reports this back to the kublet, which in go reports to Heapster.

Google's open-source ventures

Google has an assortment of open-source ventures identified with Kubernetes. Look at them, use them, and even contribute your very own code!

cAdvisor and Heapster are referenced in the following area:

cAdvisor: https://github.com/google/cadvisor

Heapster: https://github.com/kubernetes/heapster

Contrib is a trick for an assortment of segments that are not part of center

Kubernetes. It is found at:

https://github.com/kubernetes/contrib.

LevelDB is a key store library that was utilized in the production of InfluxDB. It is found at:

https://github.com/google/leveldb.

Heapster is one more open-source venture from Google; you may begin to see a topic emerging here (see the preceding information box). Heapster runs in a container on one of the minion hubs and totals the information from kublet. A basic REST interface is given to question the information.

When using the GCE arrangement, a couple of extra bundles are set up for us, which spares us time and gives us a total bundle to screen our container remaining tasks at hand. As should be obvious from the preceding System unit listing screen capture, there is another case with influx-grafana in the title.

InfluxDB is portrayed on its official site as pursues

An open-source circulated time arrangement database with no outer conditions.

InfluxDB depends on a key store bundle (allude to the past Google's open-source ventures information box) and is immaculate to store and question occasion—or time sensitive insights, for example, those gave by Heapster.

Finally, we have Grafana, which gives a dashboard and graphing interface for the information put away in InfluxDB. Using Grafana, clients can create a custom monitoring dashboard and get quick perceivability into the strength of their Kubernetes group and in this way their whole container infrastructure.

Exploring Heapster

How about we rapidly take a gander at the REST interface by running SSH to the hub with the Heapster unit.

In the first place, we can list the units to find the one running Heapster, as pursues:

$ kubectl get units - namespace=kube-system

The name of the unit should begin with monitoring-heapster. Run a depict command to see which hub it is running on, as pursues:

$ kubectl portray units/<Heapster monitoring Pod> - namespace=kube-system

From the yield in the following screen capture, we can see that the unit is running in kubernetes-minion-merd. Additionally note the IP for the unit, a couple of lines down, as we will require that in a minute:

Next, we can SSH to this container with the well-known gcloud ssh command, as pursues:

$gcloud figure - venture "<Your venture ID>" ssh - zone "<your gce zone>" "<kubernetes minion from describe>"

From here, we can get to the Heapster REST API legitimately using the case's IP address. Recall that case IPs are routable in the containers as well as on the hubs themselves. The Heapster API is listening on port 8082, and we can get a full rundown of measurements at/programming interface/v1/metric-trade pattern/.

How about we see the rundown now by issuing a twist command to the case IP address we spared from the depict command, as pursues:

$ twist - G <Heapster IP from describe>:8082/programming interface/v1/metric-send out construction/

We will see a listing that is very long. The main segment shows every one of the measurements accessible.

Customizing our dashboards

Since we have the fields, we can have a great time. Review the Grafana page we took a gander at in Chapter 1, Introduction to Kubernetes. We should pull that up again by going to our group's monitoring URL. Note that you may need to sign in with your group accreditations. Allude to the following arrangement of the link you have to utilize:

https://<your ace

IP>/programming   interface/v1/intermediary/namespaces/kube-system/ administrations/monitoring-grafana

We'll see the default Home dashboard. Snap on the down bolt beside Home and select Cluster. This shows the Kubernetes bunch dashboard, and now we can add our own measurements to the board. Look over right to the base and tap on Add a Row. This ought to create a space for another column and present a green tab on the left-hand side of the screen.

We should begin by adding a view into the filesystem use for every hub (minion). Snap on the green tab to expand and then select Add Panel and then diagram. An unfilled chart ought to show up on the screen alongside a question board for our custom diagram.

The main field in this board should show a question that starts with 'SELECT mean("value") FROM ...'. Snap on the A character beside this field to expand it. Leave the principal field beside FROM as default and then snap on the following field with the select estimation esteem. A dropdown menu will show up with the Heapster measurements we found in the past tables. Select filesystem/usage_bytes_gauge. Presently in the SELECT line, click on mean() and then on the x image to evacuate it. Next, click on the + image on the finish of the line and include selectors - > max. At that point, you'll see a GROUP BY push with time($interval) and fill(none). Cautiously click on fill and not on the (none) divide and again on x to expel it. At that point, click on the + image toward the finish of the line and select tag(hostname).

Next, how about we click on the Axes tab, with the goal that we can set the units and legend. Under Left Y Axis, click on the field alongside Unit and set it to information - > bytes and Label to Disk Space Used. Under Right Y Axis, set Unit to none - > none. Next, on the Legend tab, try to check Show in Options and Max in Values.

Presently, we should rapidly go to the General tab and pick a title. For my situation, I named mine Filesystem Disk Usage by Node (max).

We would prefer not to lose this pleasant new chart we've created, so how about we click on the spare symbol in the upper right corner. It would appear that a floppy plate (you can do a Google picture search on the off chance that you don't have a clue what this is).

After we click on the spare symbol, we will see a green exchange box that confirms the dashboard was spared. We would now be able to tap the x image over the diagram subtleties board and underneath the chart itself.

This will return us to the dashboard page. On the off chance that we look over right down, we will see our new chart. How about we add another board to this line. Again utilize the green tab and then select Add Panel - > singlestat. By and by, a vacant board will show up with a setting structure underneath it.

Suppose, we need to watch a specific hub and screen organize use. We can without much of a stretch do this by first going to the Metrics tab. At that point expand the inquiry field and set the second an incentive in the FROM field to arrange/rx. Presently we can indicate the WHERE statement by clicking the + symbol toward the finish of the line and choosing hostname from the dropdown. After hostname = click on select label esteem and pick one of the minion hubs from the rundown.

In the Options tab, ensure that Unit design is set to information - > bytes and check the Show box alongside Spark lines. The sparkline gives us a brisk history perspective on the ongoing variety in the worth. We can utilize Background mode to take up the whole foundation; of course, it utilizes the zone underneath the worth.

In Coloring, we can alternatively check the Value or Background box and pick Thresholds and Colors. This will enable us to pick different hues for the worth dependent on the edge level we indicate. Note that an unformatted form of the number must be utilized for edge esteems.

Presently, how about we return to the General tab and set the title as Network bytes got (Node35ao). Utilize the identifier for your minion hub. By and by, how about we spare our work and come back to the dashboard.

Grafana has various other board types you can play with, for example, Dashboard list, Plugin rundown, Table, and Text.

As should be obvious, it is truly simple to manufacture a custom dashboard and screen the wellbeing of our bunch initially.

FluentD and Google Cloud Logging

Looking back at the System unit listing screen capture toward the beginning of the part, you may have noticed various cases starting with the words fluentd-cloud-logging-kubernetes... . These pods show up when using the GCE supplier for your K8s bunch. A unit like this exists on each hub in our group and its sole reason for existing is to handle the processing of Kubernetes logs.

On the off chance that we sign in to our Google Cloud Platform account, we can see a portion of the logs handled there. Essentially utilize the left side, under Stackdriver select Logging. This will take us to a log listing page with various drop-down menus on the top. In the event that this is your first time visiting the page, the first dropdown will probably be set to Cloud HTTP Load Balancer.

In this drop-down menu, we'll see various GCE kinds of passages. Select GCE VM Instances and then the Kubernetes ace or one of the hubs. In the second dropdown, we can pick different log gatherings, including kublet. We can likewise channel by the occasion log level and date. Moreover, we can utilize the play catch to watch occasions stream in live:

FluentD

Presently we realize that the fluentd-cloud-logging-kubernetes units are sending the information to the Google Cloud, however for what reason do we need FluentD? Basically, FluentD is a gatherer. It very well may be designed to have different sources to gather and label logs, which are then sent to different yield points for investigation, alerting, or archiving. We can even change information using plugins before it is given to its destination.

Not all supplier arrangements have FluentD installed of course, however it is one of the prescribed ways to deal with give us more prominent adaptability for future monitoring tasks. The AWS Kubernetes arrangement likewise utilizes FluentD, however instead advances occasions to Elasticsearch.

Exploring FluentD

On the off chance that you are interested about the inner workings of the FluentD arrangement or simply need to alter the log assortment, we can investigate effectively using the kubectl executive command and one of the unit names from the command we ran before in the part.

In the first place, how about we check whether we can find the FluentD config file:

$kubectl executive fluentd-cloud-logging-kubernetes-minion-bunch r4qt -namespace=kube-system - ls/and so on/td-specialist

We will glance in the and so on organizer and then td-specialist, which is the familiar subfolder. While searching in this index, we should see a td-agent.conf file. We can see that file with a basic feline command, as pursues:

$kubectl executive fluentd-cloud-logging-kubernetes-minion-bunch r4qt -namespace=kube-system - feline/and so on/td-operator/td-agent.conf

We should see various sources including the different Kubernetes segments, Docker, and some GCP components.

While we can make changes here, recall that it is a running container and our progressions won't be spared if the unit bites the dust or is restarted. On the off chance that we truly need to alter, it's ideal to utilize this container as a base and assemble another container which we can push to a storehouse for later use.

Maturing our monitoring activities

While Grafana gives us an incredible begin to screen our container activities, it is as yet a work in progress. In this present reality of tasks, having a total dashboard see is incredible once we know there is an issue. Be that as it may, in ordinary situations, we'd like to be proactive and really get warnings when issues emerge. This kind of alerting ability is an unquestionable requirement to keep the activities group on the ball and out of receptive mode.

There are numerous arrangements accessible in this space, and we will investigate two specifically—GCE monitoring (StackDriver) and Sysdig.

GCE (StackDriver)

StackDriver is an extraordinary spot to begin for infrastructure in the general population cloud. It is really possessed by Google, so it's integrated as the Google Cloud Platform monitoring administration. Before your lock-in alerts start ringing, StackDriver likewise has strong integration with AWS. What's more, StackDriver has alerting ability with help for warning to an assortment of stages and webhooks for anything else.

Pursue GCE monitoring

In the GCE reassure, in the Stackdriver segment click on Monitoring. This will open another window, where we can pursue a free preliminary of Stackdriver. We would then be able to include our GCP venture and alternatively an AWS account also. This requires a couple of more advances, yet instructions are included on the page. Finally, we'll be given instructions on the most proficient method to install the operators on our group hubs. We can skirt this until further notice, yet will return to it in a minute.

Snap on Continue, set up your day by day alarms, and snap on Continue again.

Snap on Launch Monitoring to continue. We'll be taken to the main dashboard page, where we will see some fundamental measurements on our hub in the bunch. In the event that we select Resources from the side menu and, at that point Instances, we'll be taken to a page with every one of our hubs recorded. By clicking on the individual hub, we can again observe some essential information even without a specialist installed.

Stackdriver additionally offers monitoring and logging operators that can be installed on the hubs. In any case, it at present doesn't bolster the container OS that is utilized as a matter of course in the GCE kube-up content. You can even now observe the fundamental measurements for any hubs in GCE or AWS, however should utilize another OS on the off chance that you need the nitty gritty specialist install.

Alarms

Next, we can take a gander at the alerting arrangements accessible as a feature of the monitoring administration. From the instance subtleties page, click on the Create Alerting Policy button in the Incidents area at the highest point of the page.

We will tap on Add Condition and select a Metric Threshold. In the Target segment, set

Asset TYPE to Instance (GCE). At that point, set APPLIES to Group and kubernetes.

Leave CONDITION TRIGGERS IF set to Any Member Violates.

In the Configuration segment, leave IF METRIC as CPU Usage (GCE Monitoring) and CONDITION as above. Presently set THRESHOLD to 80 and set the time in FOR to 5 minutes.

Next, we will include a notice. In the Notification area, leave Method as Email and enter your email address.

We can avoid the Documentation area, however this is the place we can add content and formatting to alarm messages.

Finally, name the arrangement as Excessive CPU Load and tap on Save Policy.

Presently at whatever point the CPU from one of our instances goes over 80 percent, we will get an email warning. On the off chance that we ever need to audit our approaches, we can find them in the Alerting dropdown and then in Policies Overview at the menu on the left-hand side of the screen.

Past system monitoring with Sysdig

Monitoring our cloud systems is an extraordinary beginning, however shouldn't something be said about perceivability to the containers themselves? In spite of the fact that there are an assortment of cloud monitoring and perceivability instruments, Sysdig stands out for its capacity to plunge profound into system activities as well as explicitly containers.

Sysdig is open source and is charged as an all inclusive system perceivability instrument with local help for containers (you can allude to more insights concerning this in point 2 in the References area toward the finish of the section). It is a command-line apparatus, which gives insight into the zones we've taken a gander at before, for example, stockpiling, system, and system forms. What separates it is the degree of detail and perceivability it offers for these procedure and system exercises. Besides, it has local help for containers, which gives us a full image of our container tasks. This is an exceptionally prescribed device for your container tasks weapons store. The main site of Sysdig is http://www.sysdig.org/.

Sysdig Cloud

We will investigate the Sysdig instrument and a portion of the helpful command-line-based UIs in a minute. In any case, the group at Sysdig has additionally assembled a business item, named Sysdig Cloud, which gives the propelled dashboard, alerting, and warning administrations we talked about before in the section. Additionally, the differentiator here has high perceivability into containers, including some decent perceptions of our application topology.

In the event that you'd preferably skirt the Sysdig Cloud area and simply evaluate the command-line device, basically jump to the Sysdig command line segment later in this part.

On the off chance that you have not done so effectively, pursue Sysdig Cloud at http://www.sysdigcloud.com.

Subsequent to activating and logging in just because, we'll be taken to an invite page. Clicking on Next, we are indicated a page with different choices to install the sysdig operators. For our model condition, we will utilize the Kubernetes arrangement. Selecting Kubernetes will give you a page with your API key and a link to instructions. The instructions will walk you through how to create a Sysdig operator DaemonSet on your group. Remember to include the API Key from the install page.

We won't have the option to continue on the install page until the operators interface. Subsequent to creating the DaemonSet and waiting a minute, the page should continue to the AWS integration page. You can round this out in the event that you like, yet for this stroll through we will tap on Skip. At that point, click on Let's Get Started.

As of this writing, Sysdig and Sysdig Cloud were not completely good with the most recent container OS sent naturally in the GCE kube-up content, Container-Optimized OS from Google: https://cloud.google.com

/container-advanced os/docs.

We'll be taken to the main sysdig cloud dashboard screen. We should see at any rate two minion hubs show up under the Explore tab.

This page shows us a table view, and the links on the left given us a chance to investigate some key measurements for CPU, memory, networking, and so on. Despite the fact that this is an incredible beginning, the definite perspectives will give us an a lot further take a gander at every hub.

Point by point sees

We should investigate these perspectives. Select one of the minion hubs and then look down to the detail segment that shows up underneath. Of course, we should see the System: Overview by Process see (if it's not chosen, simply click on it from the rundown on the left-hand side). On the off chance that the diagram is difficult to peruse, basically utilize the boost symbol in the upper left corner of each chart for a bigger view.

There are an assortment of interesting perspectives to investigate. Just to get out a couple of others, Services | HTTP Overview and Hosts and Containers | Overview by Container give us some extraordinary diagrams for inspection. In the later view, we can see details for CPU, memory, system, and file use by container.

Topology views

Likewise, there are three topology sees at the base. These perspectives are ideal for helping us understand how our application is communicating. Snap on

Topology | Network Traffic and sit tight a couple of moments for the view to completely populate.

We note the view maps out the progression of correspondence between the minion hubs and the ace in the bunch. You may likewise take note of a + image in the top corner of the hub boxes. Snap on that in one of the minion hubs and utilize the zoom instruments at the highest point of the view zone to zoom into the subtleties

Note that we would now be able to see every one of the parts of Kubernetes running inside the ace. We can perceive how the different segments cooperate. We will see kube-intermediary and the kublet procedure running, just as various boxes with the Docker whale, which indicate that they are containers. On the off chance that we zoom in and utilize the in addition to symbol, we will see that these are the containers for our cases and center Kubernetes forms, as we found in the administrations running on the ace segment in Chapter 1, Introduction to Kubernetes.

Additionally, on the off chance that you have the ace included in your checked hubs, we can observe kublet initiate correspondence from a minion and tail it right through the kube-apiserver container in the ace.

We can even at times observe the instance correspondence with GCE infrastructure to refresh metadata. This view is incredible in request to get a psychological picture of how our infrastructure and underlying containers are talking to each other.

Measurements

Next, how about we switch over to the Metrics tab in the left-hand menu by Views. Here, there are additionally an assortment of supportive perspectives.

We should take a gander at capacity.estimated.request.total.count in System. This view shows us a gauge of what number of solicitations a hub is fit for handling when completely stacked. This can be extremely valuable for infrastructure planning:

Alerting

Since we have this extraordinary information, how about we create a few notices. Look back up to the highest point of the page and find the chime symbol by one of your minion sections. This will open a Create Alert discourse. Here, we can set manual cautions like what we did before in the part. Be that as it may, there is additionally the choice to utilize BASELINE and HOST COMPARISON.

Using the BASELINE choice is amazingly useful as Sysdig will watch the recorded examples of the hub and caution us at whatever point one of the measurements strays outside the normal metric limits. No manual settings are required, so this can truly spare time for the warning arrangement and help our tasks group to be proactive before issues emerge.

The HOST COMPARISON alternative is additionally an incredible assistance as it enables us to contrast measurements and different has and alert at whatever point one host has a metric that varies fundamentally from the gathering. An incredible use case for this is monitoring asset use crosswise over minion hubs to guarantee that our scheduling constraints are not creating a bottleneck some place in the group.

You can pick whichever alternative you like and give it a name and warning level. Empower the notice strategy. Sysdig underpins email, SNS (short for Simple Notification Service), and PagerDuty as warning techniques. You can alternatively empower Sysdig Capture to gain further insight into issues. When you have everything set, simply click on Create and you will begin to get cautions as issues come up.

The sysdig command line

Regardless of whether you just utilize the open-source instrument or you are trying out the full Sysdig Cloud bundle, the command-line utility is an incredible ally to need to find issues or get a more profound understanding of your system.

In the center instrument, there is the main sysdig utility and likewise a command-line style UI named csysdig. How about we investigate a couple of helpful commands.

Find the applicable install instructions for your OS here:

http://www.sysdig.org/install/

Once installed, allows first take a gander at the procedure with the most system action by issuing the following command:

$ sudo sysdig - pc - c topprocs_net

This is an interactive view that will show us a top procedure regarding system action. Likewise, there are a plenty of commands to use with sysdig. A couple of other helpful commands to give a shot include the following:

$sudo sysdig - pc - c topprocs_cpu

$sudo sysdig - pc - c topprocs_file

$sudo sysdig - pc - c topprocs_cpu container.name=<Container Name NOT ID>

More models can be found at

http://www.sysdig.org/wiki/sysdig-models/.

The csysdig command-line UI

Since we are in a shell on one of our hubs doesn't mean we can't have a UI. Csysdig is an adjustable UI to investigate every one of the measurements and insight that Sysdig gives. Essentially type csysdig at the brief:

$ csysdig

Subsequent to entering csysdig, we see an ongoing listing of all procedures on the machine. At the base of the screen, you'll note a menu with different choices. Snap on Views or press F2 in the event that you love to utilize your console. On the left-hand menu, there are an assortment of choices, yet we'll take a gander at strings. Double tap to choose Threads.

On some operating systems and with some SSH customers, you may have issues with the Function keys. Check the settings on your terminal and ensure the capacity keys are using the VT100+ groupings.

We can see every one of the strings at present running on the system and some information about the asset use. Of course, we see a major rundown that is updating often. On the off chance that we click on the Filter, F4 for the mouse tested, we can thin down the rundown.

Type kube-apiserver, on the off chance that you are on the ace, or kube-intermediary, in the event that you are on a hub (minion), in the channel box and press Enter.

On the off chance that we need to inspect somewhat further, we can essentially choose one of the strings in the rundown and snap on Dig or press F6. Presently we see an itemized listing of system calls from the command continuously. This can be an extremely helpful apparatus to gain profound insight into the containers and processing running on our group.

Snap on Back or press the Backspace key to return to the past screen. At that point, go to Views again. This time, we will take a gander at the Containers see. By and by, we can channel and additionally utilize the Dig view to get more top to bottom perceivability into what's going on at a system call level.

Another menu thing you may note here is Actions, which is accessible in the most up to date discharge. These highlights enable us to go from process monitoring to activity and reaction. It enables us to play out an assortment of activities from the different procedure sees in csysdig. For instance, the container see has activities to drop into a slam shell, slaughter containers, inspect logs, and more. It merits getting to know the different activities and hotkeys and even include your own custom hotkeys for regular tasks.

Prometheus

A newcomer to the monitoring scene is an open-source instrument called Prometheus. Prometheus is an open-source monitoring apparatus that was worked by a group at SoundCloud. You can find progressively about the task from https://prometheus.io.

Their site offers the following highlights (you can allude to more insights regarding this in point 3 in the References segment toward the finish of the section):

A multi-dimensional information model (time arrangement distinguished by metric name and key/esteem sets)

An adaptable inquiry language to use this dimensionality

No dependence on appropriated capacity; single server hubs are self-ruling

Time arrangement assortment happens by means of a force model over HTTP

pushing time arrangement is upheld by means of an intermediary passage

Targets are found by means of administration disclosure or static design Multiple methods of graphing and dashboard support

CoreOS has a decent blog entry on setting up Prometheus with Kubernetes here:

https://coreos.com/blog/monitoring-kubernetes-with-prometheus.html

Summary

We investigated monitoring and logging with Kubernetes. You should now be comfortable with how Kubernetes utilizes cAdvisor and Heapster to gather measurements on every one of the assets in a given bunch. Besides, we perceived how Kubernetes spares us time by providing InfluxDB and Grafana set up and arranged out of the container. Dashboards are effectively adjustable for our regular operational needs.

Moreover, we took a gander at the inherent logging abilities with FluentD and the Google Cloud Logging administration. Likewise, Kubernetes gives us incredible time savings by setting up the essentials for us.

Finally, you found out about the different outsider choices accessible to screen our containers and groups. Using these instruments will enable us to gain significantly more insight into the wellbeing and status of our applications. Every one of these devices combine to give us a strong toolset to oversee everyday activities.

In the following section, we will investigate the new group league capacities. Still for the most part in beta, this usefulness will enable us to run various bunches in different datacenters and even mists, however oversee and circulate applications from a single control plane.

Cluster Federation

This part will examine the new organization capacities and how to utilize them to deal with different groups crosswise over cloud suppliers. We will likewise cover the united variant of the center builds. We will walk you through combined Deployments, ReplicaSets, ConfigMaps, and Events.

This part will talk about the following themes:

Federating bunches

Federating different groups

Inspecting and controlling assets over different groups

Launching assets over different groups

Introduction to organization

While organization is still new in Kubernetes, it lays the preparation for the exceptionally looked for cross-cloud supplier arrangement. Using alliance, we can run different Kubernetes groups on-premise and in at least one open cloud suppliers and oversee applications utilizing the whole arrangement of all our authoritative assets.

This begins to create a way for avoiding cloud supplier lock-in and profoundly accessible sending that can put application servers in numerous bunches and take into account correspondence to different administrations situated in single points among our united groups. We can improve detachment on blackouts at a specific supplier or geographic area while providing more prominent adaptability for scaling and utilizing all out infrastructure.

At present, the league plane backings these assets (ConfigMap, DaemonSets, Deployment, Events, Ingress, Namespaces, ReplicaSets, Secrets, and Services). Note that league and its parts are in alpha and beta periods of discharge, so usefulness may in any case be somewhat touchy.

Setting up league

While we can utilize the bunch we had running for the remainder of the models, I would profoundly prescribe that you start new. The default naming of the bunches and settings can be risky for the organization system. Note that the - bunch setting and - mystery name banners are there to assist you with working around the default naming, yet for first-time alliance, it can even now be confusing and not exactly clear.

Henceforth, starting crisp is the means by which we will stroll through the models in this section. Either utilize new and separate cloud supplier (AWS and/or GCE) records or tear down the present bunch and reset your Kubernetes control condition by running the following commands:

$kubectl config unset settings

$kubectl config unset groups

Twofold watch that nothing is recorded using the following commands:

$kubectl config get-settings

$kubectl config get-bunches

Next, we will need to get the kubefed command on our way and make it executable. Explore back to the envelope where you have the Kubernetes download extricated. The kubefed command is situated in the/kubernetes/ customer/bin envelope. Run the following commands to get in the bin organizer and change the execution authorizations:

$sudo cp kubernetes/customer/bin/kubefed/usr/nearby/bin

$sudo chmod +x/usr/nearby/bin/kubefed

Settings

Settings are utilized by the Kubernetes control plane to keep confirmation and bunch setup put away for various groups. This enable us to get to and deal with numerous bunches available from the equivalent kubectl. You can generally observe the settings accessible with the get-settings command that we utilized before.

New bunches for alliance

Again, ensure you explore to any place Kubernetes was downloaded and move into the bunch sub-organizer:

$ compact disc kubernetes/group/

Before we continue, ensure you have the GCE command line and the AWS command line installed, confirmed, and arranged. Allude to Chapter 1, Introduction to Kubernetes, on the off chance that you need help doing so on another container.

In the first place, we will create the AWS bunch. Note that we are adding a situation variable named OVERRIDE_CONTEXT that will enable us to set the setting name to something that follows the DNS naming standards. DNS is a basic segment for organization as it enables us to do cross-group revelation and administration correspondence. This is significant in a unified reality where groups might be in different server farms and even suppliers.

Run these commands to create your AWS group:

$export KUBERNETES_PROVIDER=aws

$export OVERRIDE_CONTEXT=awsk8s

$./kube-up.sh

Next, we will create a GCE group, by and by using the OVERRIDE_CONTEXT condition variable:

$export KUBERNETES_PROVIDER=gce

$export OVERRIDE_CONTEXT=gcek8s

$./kube-up.sh

In the event that we investigate our settings now, we will see both the awsk8s and the gcek8s that we just created. The star before gcek8s means that it's the place kubectl is at present pointing and executing against:

$ kubectl config get-settings

Initializing the league control plane

Since we have two bunches, we should set up the alliance control plane in the GCE group. To begin with, we'll have to ensure that we are in the GCE setting, and then we will initialize the alliance control plane:

$ kubectl config use-setting gcek8s

$kubefed init ace control - have group context=gcek8s - dns-zone-name="mydomain.com"

The preceding command creates another setting only for league called ace control. It utilizes the gcek8s bunch/setting to have the league segments, (for example, API server and controller). It accept GCE DNS as the organizations DNS administration. You'll have to refresh dns-zone-name with a domain addition you oversee.

As a matter of course, the DNS supplier is GCE. You can utilize -dns-provider="aws-route53" to set it to AWS route53; be that as it may, out of the crate execution still has issues for some clients.

On the off chance that we check our settings by and by we will presently observe three settings:

$ kubectl config get-settings

How about we ensure we have all the organization segments running before we continue. The league control plane uses the alliance system namespace. Utilize the kubectl get cases command with the namespace determined to screen the advancement. When you see two API server cases and one controller unit you ought to be set:

$ kubectl get cases - namespace=federation-system

Since we have the league parts set fully operational, we should change to that setting for the subsequent stages:

$ kubectl config use-setting expert control

Adding bunches to the league system

Since we have our league control plane we can add the bunches to the alliance system. To begin with, we will join the GCE group and then the AWS bunch:

$kubefed join gcek8s - have bunch context=gcek8s - mystery name=fed-mystery gce

$kubefed join awsk8s - have bunch context=gcek8s - mystery name=fed-mystery aws

Unified assets

Unified assets enable us to convey over different groups and/or locales. As of now, adaptation 1.5 of Kubernetes bolster various center asset types in the alliance API, including ConfigMap, DaemonSets, Deployment, Events, Ingress, Namespaces, ReplicaSets, Secrets, and Services.

How about we investigate a Federated Deployment that will enable us to plan units crosswise over both

AWS and GCE:

apiVersion: augmentations/v1beta1

kind: Deployment

metadata:

name: hub js-convey

marks:

name: hub js-convey

spec:

imitations: 3

format:

metadata:

marks:

name: hub js-convey

spec:

containers:

- name: hub js-convey

picture: jonbaier/case scaling:latest ports:

- containerPort: 80

Listing 9-1. hub js-convey fed.yaml

Create this organization with the following command:

$ kubectl create - f hub js-convey fed.yaml

Presently how about we have a go at listing the cases from this organization:

$ kubectl get units

We should see a message like the preceding one portrayed. This is on the grounds that we are as yet using the ace control or organization setting, which doesn't itself run cases. We will, in any case, see the organization in the alliance plane and in the event that we inspect the occasions we will see that the sending was in certainty created on both our united groups:

$ kubectl get arrangements

$ kubectl portray arrangements hub js-convey

We should see something like the following. Notice that the Events: segment shows arrangements in both our GCE and AWS settings:

We can likewise observe the combined occasions using the following command:

$ kubectl get occasions

It might pause for a minute for every one of the three cases to run. When that occurs, we can change to each bunch setting and see a portion of the units on each. Note that we would now be able to utilize get units since we are on the individual groups and not on the control plane:

$kubectl config use-setting awsk8s

$kubectl get units

$kubectl config use-setting gcek8s

$kubectl get units

We should see the three units spread over the groups with two on one and a third on the other. Kubernetes has spread it over the group with no manual intervention. Any cases that bomb will be restarted, yet now we have the additional repetition of two cloud suppliers.

Unified designs

In present day software advancement, it isn't unexpected to isolate setup factors from the application code itself. In this manner it is simpler to make updates to support URLs, accreditations, regular ways, and so on. Having these qualities in outer arrangement files implies we can undoubtedly refresh setup without rebuilding the whole application.

This partition takes care of the initial issue, yet obvious transportability comes when you can expel the reliance from the application totally. Kubernetes offers a design store for precisely this reason. ConfigMaps are straightforward builds that store key-esteem sets.

Kubernetes likewise bolsters Secrets for increasingly touchy arrangement information. This will be shrouded in more detail in Chapter 10, Container

Security. You can utilize the model there in both single bunches or on the league control plane as we are demonstrating with ConfigMaps here.

How about we investigate a model that will enable us to store some setup and then expend it in different cases. The following listings will work for both combined and single bunches, however we will continue using a united arrangement for this model.

The ConfigMap kind can be created using strict qualities, level files and registries, and finally

YAML definition files. The following listing is a YAML definition file:

apiVersion: v1

kind: ConfigMap

metadata:

name: my-application-config

namespace: default

information:

backend-service.url: my-backend-administration

Listing 9-2: configmap-fed.yaml

Allows first switch back to our alliance plane:

$ kubectl config use-setting expert control

Presently, create this listing with the following command:

$ kubectl create - f configmap-fed.yaml

How about we show the configmap object that we just created. The - o yaml banner encourages us show the full information:

$ kubectl get configmap my-application-config - o yaml

Since we have a ConfigMap object, how about we fire up a united ReplicaSet that can utilize the ConfigMap. This will create copies of cases over our bunch that can get to

the ConfigMap object. ConfigMaps can be gotten to through condition factors or mount volumes. This model will utilize a mount volume that gives an envelope chain of command and the files for each key with the substance representing the qualities:

apiVersion: augmentations/v1beta1

kind: ReplicaSet

metadata:

name: hub js-rs

spec:

imitations: 3

selector:

matchLabels:

name: hub js-configmap-rs

format:

metadata:

marks:

name: hub js-configmap-rs

spec:

containers:

- name: configmap-case

picture: jonbaier/hub express-info:latest

ports:

- containerPort: 80

name: web

volumeMounts:

- name: configmap-volume

mountPath:/and so forth/config

volumes:

- name: configmap-volume configMap:

name: my-application-config

Listing 9-3: configmap-rs-fed.yaml

Create this case with kubectl create - f configmap-rs-fed.yaml. After creation, we

should change settings to one of the bunches where the cases are running. You can pick either, however we will utilize the GCE setting here:

$ kubectl config use-setting gcek8s

Since we are on the GCE group explicitly, we should check the configmaps here:

$ kubectl get configmaps

As should be obvious, the ConfigMap is spread locally to each bunch. Next, how about we find a case from our combined ReplicaSet:

$ kubectl get cases

How about we take one of the hub js-rs case names from the listing and run a slam shell with kubectl executive:

$ kubectl executive - it hub js-rs-6g7nj slam

At that point change registries to the/and so forth/config organizer that we set up in the case definition. Listing this index uncovers a single file with the name of the ConfigMap we defined before:

$cd/and so on/config

$ls

In the event that we, at that point show the substance of the files with the following command, we should see the worth we entered before: my-backend-administration:

$ reverberation $(cat backend-service.url)

If we somehow happened to glance in any of the units over our combined group we would see similar qualities. This is an extraordinary method to decouple arrangement from an application and appropriate it over our armada of bunches.

Other unified assets

So far we saw unified Deployments, ReplicaSets, Events, and ConfigMaps in

activity. DaemonSets, Ingress, Namespaces, Secrets, and Services are additionally upheld. Your particular arrangement will fluctuate and you may have a lot of bunches that vary from our model here. As referenced before, these assets are still in beta, so it merits spending some an opportunity to explore different avenues regarding the different asset types and understand how well the league develops are upheld for your specific blend of infrastructure.

Genuine multi-cloud

This is an exciting space to watch. As it develops it gives us a great beginning to doing multi-cloud usage and providing excess crosswise over districts, server farms, and even cloud suppliers.

While Kubernetes provides a simple and exciting way to multi-cloud infrastructure, note that generation multi-cloud requires significantly more than dispersed organizations. A full arrangement of abilities from logging and monitoring to consistence and host-hardening, there is a lot to oversee in a multi-supplier arrangement.

Genuine multi-cloud selection will require a well-arranged design, and Kubernetes steps forward in pursuing this objective.

Summary

In this section, we took a gander at the new league abilities in Kubernetes. We perceived how we can send groups to various cloud suppliers and oversee them from a single control plane. We additionally conveyed an application crosswise over groups in both AWS and GCE. While these highlights are new and still mainly in alpha and beta, we should now have the right stuff to use them as they advance and become some portion of the standard Kubernetes operating model.

In the following part, we will investigate another propelled point, security. We will cover the nuts and bolts for secure containers and likewise how to verify your Kubernetes group. We will likewise take a gander at the Secrets build, which gives us the capacity to store touchy setup information like our preceding ConfigMap model.

Container Security

This section will examine the essentials of holder security from the compartment runtime level to the host itself. We will talk about how to apply these ideas to remaining tasks at hand running in a Kubernetes bunch and a portion of the security concerns and practices that relate explicitly to running your Kubernetes group.

This part will examine the accompanying themes:

Fundamental holder security

Holder picture security and ceaseless powerlessness filtering

Kubernetes bunch security

Kubernetes mysteries

Nuts and bolts of holder security

Holder security is a profound branch of knowledge and in itself can fill its very own book. Having said this, we will cover a portion of the elevated level concerns and give a beginning stage to consider this zone.

In the A short diagram of holders area of Chapter 1, Introduction to Kubernetes, we took a gander at a portion of the center segregation includes in the Linux part that empower compartment innovation. Understanding the subtleties of how compartments work is the way to getting a handle on the different security worries in overseeing them.

Keeping compartments contained

One of the most clear highlights talked about in the paper is that of getting away from the seclusion/virtualization of the compartment develop. Current holder usage watch against this utilizing namespaces to detach forms just as permitting control of the Linux abilities accessible to a compartment. Also, there is an expanded move towards secure default arrangements of the out-of-the-case compartment condition. For instance,

Docker as a matter of course just empowers a little arrangement of capacities (you can allude to more subtleties about this in point 2 in the References segment toward the finish of the section). Systems administration is another road of break and it very well may be trying since there are an assortment of system

choices that fitting in to most present day holder arrangements.

The following zone examined in the paper is that of assaults between two holders. The User namespace model gives us included assurance here by mapping the root client inside the holder to a lower level client on the host machine. Systems administration is obviously still an issue and something that requires appropriate constancy and consideration while choosing and actualizing your holder organizing arrangement.

Assaults inside the holder itself are another vector and likewise with past concerns, namespaces and organizing are critical to security here. Another perspective that is imperative in this situation is simply the application security. The code still needs to pursue secure coding rehearses and the software ought to be stayed up with the latest and fixed consistently. At long last, the productivity of holder images has an additional advantage of contracting the assault surface. The images ought to be worked with just the bundles and software essential.

Asset fatigue and arrangement security

Like the Denial of Service assaults, we've seen in different territories of figuring that asset weariness is especially a relevant worry in the holder world. While cgroups give a few impediments on asset use for things, for example, CPU, memory, and plate use, there are as yet substantial assault roads for asset depletion. Devices, for example, Docker offer some beginning defaults to the cgroups confinements, and Kubernetes likewise offers extra restricts that can be set on gatherings of compartments running in the bunch. It's essential to understand these defaults and change for your organizations.

While the Linux part and the highlights that empower holders give us some type of detachment, they are genuinely new to the Linux working system. All things considered, despite everything they contain their own bugs and vulnerabilities. The inherent systems for abilities and namespaces can and do have issues and it is critical to follow these as a feature of your protected holder activities.

The last region shrouded in the NCC paper is simply the assault of the compartment the board layer itself. The Docker motor, picture repositories, and arrangement instruments are largely huge vectors of assault and ought to be viewed as when building up your methodology. We'll glance more inside and out at how we can address the repositories and Kubernetes as a coordination layer in the following areas.

In case you're keen on find out about the particular security highlights of Docker's execution, investigate:

https://docs.docker.com/motor/security/security/.

Picture repositories

Helplessness the executives is a basic segment of any cutting edge IT activity. Zero-day vulnerabilities are on the ascent and even those vulnerabilities with patches can be unwieldy to remediate. To start with, application proprietors must be made mindful of their vulnerabilities and potential patches. At that point these patches must be coordinated into systems and code and often this requires extra arrangements or support windows. In any event, when there is perceivability to vulnerabilities, there is often a slack in remediation, often taking enormous associations a while to fix.

While holders significantly improve the way toward refreshing applications and limiting personal time, there still stays a test innate in weakness the executives. Particularly since an aggressor just needs to uncover one such weakness; making anything short of 100% of systems fixed is a hazard for bargain.

What's required is a quicker criticism circle in addressing vulnerabilities. Constant filtering and integrating with the software arrangement life cycle is critical to speeding the data and remediation of vulnerabilities. Fortunately, this is actually the methodology being incorporated with the most recent holder the board and security tooling.

Persistent helplessness examining

One such open-source venture that has developed in this space is Clair. We become acquainted with this from the Clair GitHub page: Clair is an open source venture for the static investigation of vulnerabilities in appc and docker holders.

You can visit Clair at the accompanying connection:

https://github.com/coreos/clair.

Clair examines your code against Common Vulnerabilities and Exploits (CVEs). It tends to be coordinated into your CI/CD pipeline and run as a reaction to new forms. In the event that vulnerabilities are discovered, they can be taken as input into the pipeline, even stop arrangement, and bomb the construct. This powers designers to know about and remediate vulnerabilities during their typical discharge process.

Clair can be incorporated with various compartment picture repositories and CI/CD pipelines.

Clair can even be sent on Kubernetes: https://github.com/coreos/clair#kubernetes.

Clair is additionally utilized as the filtering system in CoreOS's Quay picture store. Quay offers various undertaking highlights including ceaseless helplessness checking:

https://quay.io/

Both Docker Hub and Docker Cloud bolster security checking. Once more, compartments that are pushed to the storehouse are consequently filtered against CVEs and warnings of vulnerabilities are sent because of any discoveries. Also, parallel examination of the code is performed to coordinate the mark of the segments with that of known renditions.

There are an assortment of other checking instruments that can be utilized also for filtering your picture repositories including OpenSCAP just as Twistlock and AquaSec

Picture marking and check

Regardless of whether you are utilizing a private picture vault in-house or an open repo, for example, Docker Hub, realize that you are running just the code that your engineers have composed. The potential for pernicious code or man-in-the-center assaults on downloads is a significant factor in securing your compartment images.

Accordingly, both rkt and Docker bolster the capacity to sign images and confirm that the substance have not changed. Distributers can utilize keys to sign the images when they are pushed to the repositories and clients can confirm the mark on the client-side when downloading for use:

From the rkt documentation:

"Before executing a remotely brought ACI, rkt will confirm it dependent on appended marks produced by the ACI maker."

https://coreos.com/rkt/docs/most recent/subcommands/trust.ht ml

https://coreos.com/rkt/docs/most recent/marking and-verifica tion-guide.html

From the Docker documentation:

"Content trust enables you to confirm both the honesty and the distributer of the considerable number of information got from a library over any channel."

https://docs.docker.com/motor/security/trust/content_t rust/

From the Docker Notary GitHub page:

"The Notary venture includes a server and a client for running and collaborating with confided in assortments."

https://github.com/docker/public accountant

Kubernetes group security

Kubernetes has kept on including various security includes in their most recent discharges and has a balanced arrangement of control focuses that can be utilized in your bunch; everything from secure node correspondence to unit security and even capacity of delicate design information.

Secure API calls

During each apus call, Kubernetes applies various security controls.

After secure TLS correspondence is built up, the API server goes through Authorization and Authentication. At long last, an Admission Controller circle is applied to the solicitation before it arrives at the API server.

Secure node correspondence

Kubernetes bolsters the utilization of secure correspondence channels between the API server and any client including the nodes themselves. Regardless of whether it's a GUI or command-line utility, for example, kubectl, we can utilize authentications to speak with the API server. Consequently, the API server is the focal communication point for any progressions to the group and is a basic part to verify.

In organizations, for example, GCE, the kubelet on every node is conveyed for secure correspondence as a matter of course. This arrangement utilizes the TLS bootstrapping and the new testaments' API to set up a protected association with the API server utilizing TLS client endorsements and a Certificate Authority (CA) bunch.

Approval and validation modules

The module systems for validation and approval in Kubernetes are in their early stages. Be that as it may, these highlights likewise keep on creating in the following barely any discharges. There are likewise outsider suppliers that incorporate with the highlights here.

Verification is at present bolstered as tokens, passwords, and authentications with plans to include the module ability at a later stage. OpenID Connect tokens are upheld and a few outsider usage, for example, Dex from CoreOS and aser record and validation from Cloud Foundry, are accessible.

Approval as of now underpins three modes. The full RBAC (short for Role-Based Access Control)mode is as yet a work in advance and will in the end bring a develop job based confirmation from Kubernetes itself. Quality Based Access Control (ABAC) is as of now upheld and gives a client a chance to characterize benefits by means of traits in a file. At long last, a webhook system is bolstered, which considers mix with outsider approval by means of REST web administration calls.

Get familiar with every territory here:

http://kubernetes.io/docs/administrator/approval/http://kubernetes.io/docs/administrator/verification/

Confirmation controllers

Kubernetes likewise gives a system to coordinating with extra check as a last advance. This could be as picture examining, signature checks, or anything that can react in the predetermined style. At the point when an API call is made, the snare is called and that server can run its confirmation. Confirmation controllers can likewise be utilized to change asks for and include or modify the first solicitation. When the tasks are run, a reaction is then sent back with a status that teaches Kubernetes to permit or deny the call.

This can be particularly useful for checking or testing images as we referenced in the last area. The ImagePolicyWebhook module gives a confirmation controller that takes into account joining with extra picture assessment.

For more data, visit the Using Admission Controller page in the accompanying documentation:

https://kubernetes.io/docs/administrator/affirmation controllers/.

Case security strategies and setting

Probably the most recent expansion to the Kubernetes' security munititions stockpile is that of Pod security approaches and settings. These enable clients to control clients and gatherings for holder forms and appended volumes, limit the utilization of host systems or namespaces, and even set the root filesystem to peruse as it were. Furthermore, we can confine the capacities accessible and likewise set SELinux alternatives for the names that are applied to the holders in each unit.

Notwithstanding SELinux, Kubernetes likewise included help for utilizing AppArmor with your cases utilizing comments. For more data, allude to the accompanying documentation page:

https://kubernetes.io/docs/administrator/apparmor/.

We'll stroll through a case of utilizing a case security setting to add a few imperatives to our units. Since the usefulness is still in beta, we'll have to empower the beta augmentations API and likewise add PodSecurityPolicy to the rundown of affirmation controllers being used.

Empowering beta APIs

To start with, you'll have to SSH into your lord node, change to a root client, and then alter the

/and so forth/kubernetes/shows/kube-apiserver.manifest file in your favored supervisor. Once more, we can SSH by means of the Google Cloud CLI or utilize the Google Cloud Console, which has a worked in SSH client on the VM occasions page.

The best practice isn't to SSH onto the nodes themselves. Notwithstanding, we have done as such at a few points in this book for illustrative purposes. It's imperative to understand how things are running on the nodes themselves and can here and there be essential both for learning and investigating. Having said this, utilization the instruments, for example, kubectl executive when you essentially need to run a command from inside the bunch or a unit.

Look down to the command segment and we should see something like the accompanying posting:

"canister/sh",

"- c",

"/usr/neighborhood/canister/kube-apiserver - v=2 - cloud-config=/and so on/gce.conf -

address=127.0.0.1 - permit

privileged=true - approval strategy file=/and so on/srv/kubernetes/abac-authz-policy.jsonl - essential auth-file=/and so on/srv/kubernetes/basic_auth.csv - cloud-provider=gce - client-ca-file=/and so on/srv/kubernetes/ca.crt - etcd-servers=http://127.0.0.1:2379 -

etcd-servers-overrides=/events#http://127.0.0.1:4002 - secure-port=443 - tls-cert-file=/and so forth

/srv/kubernetes/server.cert - tls-private-key-

file=/and so forth/srv/kubernetes/server.key - token-auth-

file=/and so forth/srv/kubernetes/known_tokens.csv - capacity backend=etcd2 - target-

slam mb=180 - administration group ip-range=10.0.0.0/16 - etcd-majority read=false

- affirmation

control=NamespaceLifecycle,LimitRanger,ServiceAccount,PersistentVolumeLabel

,DefaultStorageClass,ResourceQuota

- approval mode=ABAC - permit privileged=true 1>>/var/log/ kube-apiserver.log 2>&1"

Your posting may shift, so simply include the parameters featured in striking as pursues. Additionally, duplicate the first posting as a reinforcement so you can reestablish it if necessary later on:

"container/sh",

"- c",

"/usr/neighborhood/container/kube-apiserver - v=2 - cloud-config=/and so forth/gce.conf - address=127.0.0.1

- permit privileged=true - approval arrangement

file=/and so forth/srv/kubernetes/abac-authz-policy.jsonl - fundamental auth-

file=/and so forth/srv/kubernetes/basic_auth.csv - cloud-provider=gce - client-ca-file=/and so forth/srv/kubernetes/ca.crt - etcd-servers=http://127.0.0.1:2379 -

etcd-servers-overrides=/events#http://127.0.0.1:4002 - secure-port=443 -

tls-cert-file=/and so forth/srv/kubernetes/server.cert - tls-private-key-

file=/and so forth/srv/kubernetes/server.key - token-auth-

file=/and so forth/srv/kubernetes/known_tokens.csv - capacity backend=etcd2 - target-

slam mb=180 - administration group ip-range=10.0.0.0/16 - etcd-majority read=false

- affirmation

control=NamespaceLifecycle,LimitRanger,ServiceAccount,PersistentVolumeLabe

,DefaultStorageClass,ResourceQuota,PodSecurityPolicy - approval

mode=ABAC - permit privileged=true - runtime-

config=extensions/v1beta1=true,extensions/v1beta1/
podsecuritypolicy=true

1>>/var/log/kube-apiserver.log 2>&1"

Spare the file and exit sudo on the off chance that you have a root shell. In the event that all goes well, Kubernetes should see the show changes and restart the API Server. This may take a couple of moments and during reboot, kubectl may get lethargic. I for the most part watch this with the accompanying command:

$ kubectl get cases - namespace=kube-system

Watch the STATUS and AGE sections. Once the restart is fruitful, we'll have a STATUS of Running and an AGE on the request for a couple of moments or less.

On the off chance that we had any grammatical errors with the show, we may see blunders in STATUS or even get a for all time inert kubectl. On the off chance that this occurs, we'll have to reestablish our prior parameters. As a last resort, you can reboot the case. The default for GCE arrangements has a boot content that will supplant the show with the default settings.

When your API server is refreshed and running, we can include a security approach and run a unit with a case security setting characterized. The arrangement runs at the bunch level and implements the strategy for all units. The unit security setting is set in the case definition and applies just to that case.

Making a PodSecurityPolicy

Since we've included the PodSecurityPolicy confirmation controller, we'll have to include a case security approach before we can create our model in posting 10-2 further down.

Once more, the case security approach applies group wide:

{

"kind": "PodSecurityPolicy",

"apiVersion":"extensions/v1beta1",

"metadata": {

"name": "default"

},

"spec": {

"special": bogus,

"seLinux": {

"rule": "RunAsAny"

```json
        },
        "supplementalGroups": {
            "rule": "RunAsAny"
        },
        "runAsUser": {
            "rule": "RunAsAny"
        },
        "fsGroup": {
            "rule": "RunAsAny"
        },
        "volumes": ["*"],
        "readOnlyRootFilesystem": genuine
    }
}
```

Posting 10-1: default-security-policy.json

Create this with the accompanying:

```
$ kubectl create - f default-security-policy.json
```

The previous default approach doesn't enable compartments to run in special mode. It permits any seLinux names, any supplemental gathering IDs, any client to run the main procedure, and any gathering ID for the filesytems. It additionally bolsters a wide range of volumes.

Since we have a fundamental approach for the group, how about we create a Pod. To start with, we will create a Pod with our node-express-information compartment:

apiVersion: v1

kind: Pod

metadata:

name: node-js-nopsc

spec:

holders:

- name: node-js-nopsc

picture: jonbaier/node-express-info:latest ports:

- containerPort: 80

Posting 10-2: nodejs-case nopsc.yaml

Create the case with the former posting. At that point utilize the kubectl executive command to get a shell inside the case. Next, we will endeavor to create a file utilizing the touch command:

$kubectl executive - it node-js-nopsc slam

root@node-js-nopsc:/src# contact file.txt

We ought to get a blunder like touch: can't contact 'file.txt': Read-just file system. This is on the grounds that we set the ReadOnlyFileSystem property to genuine, so all holders (unit security setting characterized or not) are currently run with read-just root filesystems. Type exit to leave this case.

Making a case with a PodSecurityContext

Since we have seen the impacts of the unit security strategy, we should investigate the case security setting. Here we can characterize seLinuxOptions that let us characterize the name setting for the holders in the unit. We can likewise characterize runAsUser to indicate the UID with which every compartment will run and the runAsNonRoot banner that will basically anticipate beginning holders that run as UID 0 or root. We can likewise determine the Group (GID) for the primary procedure in every holder with supplementalGroup. At long last, we can indicate the Group (GID) for filesystem proprietorship and new files with fsGroup.

Posting 10-4 is a rendition of our past node-express-information unit with the runAsNonRoot set to genuine. Understand that root (UID 0) is the default client if none is characterized in the Dockerfile. Posting 10-3 shows the Dockerfile for our node-express-information compartment. We have not characterized the USER mandate and along these lines it will run as root:

FROM node:latest

Include src//src

WORKDIR/src

RUN npm introduce

ENV PORT=80

CMD ["node", "index.js"]

Posting 10-3: node-express-data Dockerfile

apiVersion: v1

kind: Pod

metadata:

name: node-js-case

spec:

holders:

- name: node-js-case

picture: jonbaier/node-express-info:latest ports:

- containerPort: 80

securityContext:

runAsNonRoot: genuine

Posting 10-4: nodejs-case psc.yaml

Understanding the connection between the security setting and how the holders are fabricated is significant. On the off chance that we attempt to create the former Listing 10-4 with kubectl create - f nodejs-case psc.yaml, we will see that it never starts and gives us

VerifyNonRootError:

Understanding that running holders safely is anything but a simply an assignment of executives including imperatives is significant. The work must be done as a team with engineers who will appropriately create the images.

Tidy up

The arrangement we have set up might be unreasonably prohibitive for learning and improvement, so you may wish to expel it. You can do as such with the accompanying command:

$ kubectl erase psp default

You'll likewise need to fix the progressions to /and so on/kubernetes/shows/ kube-apiserver.manifest that we did on the Kubernetes ace toward the start of this segment. In particular, you should expel the PodSecurityPolicy from the rundown of the confirmation control area.

Extra contemplations

Notwithstanding the highlights we just assessed, Kubernetes has various different develops that ought to be considered in your general bunch solidifying process. Prior in the book, we took a gander at namespaces that give a legitimate partition to multi-tenure. While the namespaces themselves don't segregate the real system traffic, a portion of the system modules, for example, Calico and Canal, give extra ability to organize approaches. We additionally took a gander at portions and constrains that can be set for each namespace and ought to be utilized to keep a solitary occupant or undertaking from expending such a large number of assets inside the bunch.

Verifying touchy application information (insider facts)

At times, our application needs to hold touchy data. This can be qualifications or tokens to sign in to a database or administration. Putting away this delicate data in the picture itself is something to be kept away from. Here, Kubernetes gives us an answer in the develop of insider facts.

Privileged insights give us an approach to store touchy data without incorporating plaintext forms in our asset definition files. Privileged insights can be mounted to the cases that need them and then got to inside the unit as files with the mystery esteems as substance. On the other hand, you can likewise uncover the privileged insights through condition factors.

We can without much of a stretch create a mystery either with YAML or on the command line. Privileged insights do should be base-64 encoded, however on the off chance that we utilize the kubectl command line, this encoding is accomplished for us.

How about we start with the accompanying Secret:

$kubectl create mystery conventional mystery phrases -from-literal=quiet-phrase="Shh! Dont' tell"

We would then be able to check for the Secret with this command:

$ kubectl get insider facts

Since we have effectively created the Secret, how about we make a case that can utilize the mystery. Privileged insights are devoured in units by method for joined volumes. In the accompanying Listing 10-5, you'll see that we use volumeMount to mount the key to an organizer in our compartment:

apiVersion: v1

kind: Pod

metadata:

name: mystery case

spec:

holders:

- name: mystery case

picture: jonbaier/node-express-info:latest ports:

- containerPort: 80

name: web

volumeMounts:

- name: mystery volume

mountPath:/and so forth/mystery phrases

volumes:

- name: mystery volume mystery:

secretName: mystery phrases

Posting 10-5: mystery pod.yaml

Create this case with kubectl create - f mystery pod.yaml. Once created, we can get a slam shell in the unit with kubectl executive and then change indexes to the/and so on/mystery phrases envelope that we set up in the case definition. Posting this catalog uncovers a solitary file with the name of the mystery that we created before:

$kubectl executive - it mystery case slam

$cd/and so forth/mystery phrases

$ls

On the off chance that we, at that point show those substance, we should see the expression we encoded beforehand, Shh!

Dont' tell:

$ feline calm expression

Normally, this would be utilized for a username and secret word to a database or administration, or any delicate accreditations and arrangement information.

Remember that privileged insights are still in their beginning times, however they are an indispensable segment for creation activities. There are a few upgrades arranged here for future discharges. Right now, mysteries are still put away in plaintext in the etcd server. Be that as it may, the privileged insights develop allows us to control which units can get to it and it stores the data on the tmpfs, yet doesn't store it very still for each case. You'll likely need more security set up for a generation prepared system.

Summary

We investigated fundamental holder security and some basic territories of thought. We additionally addressed essential picture security and consistent helplessness checking. Later in this section, we took a gander at the general security highlights of Kubernetes including insider facts for putting away touchy setup information, secure API calls, and in any event, setting up security arrangements and settings for cases running on our group.

You should now have a strong beginning stage for verifying your group and moving towards creation. Keeping that in mind, the following section will cover a general technique for moving towards generation and will likewise take a gander at some outsider merchants that offer instruments to fill in the holes and help you in transit.

Extending Kubernetes with OCP, CoreOS, and Tectonic

The primary portion of this part will cover how open standards empower a differing ecosystem of compartment usage. We'll take a gander at the Open Container Initiative (OCI) and its crucial give an open holder determination also. The second 50% of this section will cover CoreOS and its preferences as a host OS, including execution and backing for different compartment usage. Additionally, we'll investigate the Tectonic undertaking offering from CoreOS.

This section will talk about the accompanying subjects:

Why standards matter?

The Open Container Initiative and Cloud Native Computing Foundation

Compartment details versus usage

CoreOS and its points of interest

Structural

The significance of standards

In the course of recent years, containerization innovation has had an enormous development in fame. While Docker has been at the focal point of this ecosystem, there is an expanded number of players in the compartment space. There is as of now various options in contrast to the containerization and Docker execution itself (rkt, Garden, and so on). Also, there is a rich ecosystem of outsider apparatuses that upgrade and praise your holder framework. Kubernetes lands unequivocally on the organization side of this ecosystem, however most importantly every one of these apparatuses structure the premise to construct cloud-local applications.

As we referenced at the absolute starting point of the book, a most alluring aspect concerning compartments is their capacity to bundle our application for sending across different condition levels (that is, improvement, trying, and generation) and different foundation suppliers (GCP, AWS, On-premise, and so on).

To genuinely bolster this sort of organization dexterity, we need not just the compartments themselves to have a typical stage, yet in addition the fundamental details to pursue a typical arrangement of standard procedures. This will take into consideration executions that are both adaptable and profoundly specific. For instance, a few remaining tasks at hand may should be run on a profoundly secure execution. To give this, the execution should settle on increasingly purposeful choices about certain parts of usage. In either case, we will have greater nimbleness and opportunity if our compartments are based on some normal structures that all usage concur on and support.

The Open Container Initiative

One of the principal activities to increase boundless industry commitment is the OCI. Among the 36 business partners are Docker, Red Hat, VMware, IBM, Google, and AWS, and they are recorded on the OCI site at:

https://www.opencontainers.org/.

The motivation behind the OCI is to part executions, for example, Docker and rkt, from a standard particular for the configuration and runtime of containerized remaining tasks at hand. By their very own terms, the objective of the OCI particular has three fundamental tenets(you can allude to more insights regarding this in point 1 in the References area toward the finish of the section):

Making a proper determination for holder picture positions and runtime, which will enable an agreeable compartment to be compact across all major, consistent working systems and stages without fake specialized hindrances.

Tolerating, keeping up, and propelling the ventures related with these standards (the Projects). It will hope to concur on a standard arrangement of compartment activities (start, executive, pause,....) just as runtime condition related with compartment runtime.

Blending the already referenced standard with other proposed standards, including the appc particular.

Cloud Native Computing Foundation

A second activity that additionally has a far reaching industry acknowledgment is the Cloud Native Computing Foundation (CNCF). While still centered around containerized outstanding burdens, the CNCF works somewhat higher up the stack at an application configuration level. The reason for existing is to give a standard arrangement of instruments and innovations to manufacture, work, and coordinate cloud-local application stacks. Cloud has given us access to an assortment of new advances and practices that can improve and advance our exemplary software structures. This is additionally especially centered at the new worldview of microservice-arranged improvement.

As an establishing member in CNCF, Google has given the Kubernetes open-source venture as the initial step. The objective will be to expand interoperability in the ecosystem and bolster better incorporation with ventures. CNCF is now facilitating an assortment of undertakings in arrangement, logging, checking, following, and application strength.

For more data on CNCF, allude to https://cncf.io/.

Standard holder determination

A center aftereffect of the OCI exertion is the creation and improvement of the all-encompassing holder detail. The determination has five center standards for all compartments to pursue, which I will quickly summarize (you can allude to more insights regarding this in point 2 in the References area toward the finish of the section):

The holder must have standard tasks to create, start, and stop compartments across all executions.

The compartment must be content-freethinker, which implies that kind of utilization inside the holder doesn't change the standard tasks or distributing of the holder itself.

The compartment must be foundation skeptic too. Versatility is principal; in this manner, the holders must have the option to work simply in GCE as in your organization's datacenter or on a designer's PC.

A holder should likewise be intended for computerization, which enables us to robotize across the manufacture, refreshing, and arrangement pipelines. While this standard is somewhat dubious, the compartment execution ought not require difficult manual strides for creation and discharge.

At long last, the usage must help modern evaluation conveyance. Indeed, addressing the fabricate and arrangement pipelines and requiring a streamlined proficiency to the versatility and travel of the compartments among foundation and organization levels.

The particular likewise characterizes center standards for holder groups and runtimes. You can peruse increasingly about the particulars on the GitHub venture at https://github.com/opencontainers/specs.

While the center determination can be somewhat dynamic, the runC usage is a solid case of the OCI specs as a compartment runtime and picture position. Once more, you can peruse a greater amount of the specialized subtleties on the runC site and GitHub at the accompanying URLs: https://github.com/opencontainers/runc https://runc.io/

The sponsorship group and runtime for an assortment of well known compartment apparatuses is runC. It was given to OCI by Docker and was created from a similar pipes work utilized in the Docker stage. Since its discharge, it has had an invite take-up by various undertakings.

Indeed, even the prevalent open source PaaS, Cloud Foundry reported that it will utilize runC in Garden. Nursery gives the containerization pipes to Deigo, which goes about as a coordination layer like Kubernetes.

The rkt execution was initially founded on the appc particular. The appc particular was really a previous endeavor by the people at CoreOS to frame a typical determination around containerization. Presently that CoreOS is taking an interest in OCI, they are attempting to help blend the appc determination into OCI; it should bring about a more significant level of similarity across the holder ecosystem.

CoreOS

While the details give us a shared opinion, there are additionally a few patterns developing around the decision of OS for our compartments. There are a few tailor-fit OSes that are being grown explicitly to run holder outstanding tasks at hand. In spite of the fact that usage differ, they all have comparative qualities. Concentrate on a thin establishment base, nuclear OS refreshing, and marked applications for productive and secure activities.

One OS that is picking up ubiquity is CoreOS. CoreOS offers significant benefits for both security and asset usage. It gives asset usage by expelling bundle conditions totally from the image. Rather, CoreOS runs all applications and administrations in compartments. By giving just a little arrangement of administrations required to help running compartments and bypassing the need of hypervisor utilization, CoreOS gives us a chance to utilize a bigger bit of the asset pool to run our containerized applications. This enables clients to increase a better from their framework and better compartment to node (server) use proportions.

More holder OSes

There are a few other holder streamlined OSes that have risen as of late.

Red Hat Enterprise Linux Atomic Host centers around security with SELinux empowered as a matter of course and Atomic updates to the OS like what we saw with CoreOS. Allude to the accompanying connection:

https://access.redhat.com/articles/rhel-nuclear beginning

Ubuntu Snappy additionally benefits from the productivity and security increases of isolating the OS segments from the structures and applications. Utilizing application images and check marks, we get a proficient Ubuntu-based OS for our holder remaining tasks at hand at http://www.ubuntu.com

/cloud/instruments/smart.

Ubuntu LXD runs a compartment hypervisor and gives a way to moving Linux-based VMs to holders effortlessly:

https://www.ubuntu.com/cloud/lxd.

VMware Photon is another lightweight compartment OS that is enhanced explicitly for vSphere and the VMware stage. It runs Docker, rkt, and Garden and additionally has a few images that you can run on the well known open cloud suppliers. Allude to the accompanying connection:

https://vmware.github.io/photon/.

At long last, CoreOS has some additional preferences in the domain of security. First off, the OS can be refreshed as one entire unit rather than by means of individual bundles (allude to the previous figure). This keeps away from numerous issues that emerge from halfway updates. To accomplish this, CoreOS utilizes two allotments—one as the dynamic OS parcel and an auxiliary one to get a full update. When updates are finished effectively, a reboot advances the auxiliary segment. In the case of anything turns out badly, the first parcel is accessible for failback.

The system proprietors can likewise control when those updates are applied. This gives us the adaptability to organize basic updates while working with genuine planning for the more typical updates. Likewise, the whole update is marked and transmitted through SSL for included security across the whole procedure.

rkt

A focal bit of the CoreOS ecosystem is its very own holder runtime, named rkt. As we referenced before, rkt is another execution with a particular spotlight on security. The principle preferred position of rkt is in running the motor without a daemon as root, the manner in which Docker does today. At first, rkt likewise had a favorable position in setting up a trust for holder images. Be that as it may, late updates to Docker have made incredible steps with the new Content Trust include.

Most importantly rkt is as yet an execution concentrated on security to run holders underway. rkt uses a picture design named ACI, yet it additionally bolsters running Docker-based images. Over the previous year, rkt has experienced huge updates and is currently at form 1.24.0. It has increased a lot of energy as an approach to run Docker images safely underway.

Also, CoreOS is working with Intel® to incorporate the new Intel® Virtualization Technology, which enables compartments to run in more elevated levels of segregation. This equipment improved security enables the holders to be run inside a Kernel-based Virtual Machine (KVM) process giving segregation from the piece like what we see with hypervisors today.

etcd

Another focal piece in the CoreOS ecosystem worth referencing is their open-source etcd venture. etcd is a conveyed and predictable key-esteem store. A RESTful API is utilized to interface with etcd, so it's anything but difficult to incorporate with your task.

On the off chance that it sounds natural, this is on the grounds that we saw this procedure running in Chapter 1, Introduction to Kubernetes, in the Services running on the ace area. Kubernetes really uses etcd to monitor group setup and current state. K8s utilizes it for the administration disclosure capacities also. For more subtleties, allude to https://github.com/coreos/etcd.

Kubernetes with CoreOS

Since we understand the benefits, we should investigate a Kubernetes bunch utilizing CoreOS. The documentation underpins various stages, however one of the least demanding to turn up is AWS with the CoreOS CloudFormation and CLI contents.

On the off chance that you are keen on running Kubernetes with CoreOS on different stages, you can discover more subtleties in the CoreOS documentation at

https://coreos.com/kubernetes/docs/most recent/.

We can locate the most recent guidelines for AWS at https://coreos.com/kubernetes/docs/most recent/kubernetes-on-aws.ht ml.

You can adhere to the guidelines referenced before to turn up Kubernetes on CoreOS. You'll have to create a key pair on AWS and likewise determine a district, group name, bunch size, and DNS to continue.

Also, we should create a DNS passage and will require an assistance, for example, Route53 or a generation DNS administration. When adhering to the guidelines, you'll need to set the DNS to a space or sub-area, where you have authorization to establish up a precedent. We should refresh the record after the bunch is ready for action and has a powerful endpoint characterized.

There you have it! We presently have a bunch running CoreOS. The content creates all the fundamental AWS assets, for example, Virtual Private Clouds (VPCs), security gatherings, and IAM job. Since the bunch is going we can get the endpoint with the status command and update our DNS record:

$ kube-aws status

Duplicate the section recorded alongside Controller DNS Name and then alter your DNS records to point the area or sub-space you indicated prior to point to this heap balancer.

In the event that you overlook which space you determined or need to keep an eye on the design you can glance in the produced kubeconifg file with your preferred supervisor. It will look something like this:

apiVersion: v1

kind: Config

bunches:

- bunch:

authentication authority: qualifications/ca.pem

server: https://coreos.mydomain.com

name: kube-aws-my-coreos-bunch group

settings:

- setting:

bunch: kube-aws-my-coreos-group bunch

namespace: default

client: kube-aws-my-coreos-bunch administrator

name: kube-aws-my-coreos-bunch setting

clients:

- name: kube-aws-my-coreos-bunch administrator

client:

client-authentication: qualifications/admin.pem

client-key: accreditations/administrator key.pem

current-setting: kube-aws-my-coreos-bunch setting

For this situation, the server line will have your area name.

On the off chance that this is a crisp box, you should download kubectl independently as it isn't packaged with kube-aws:

$ wget

https://storage.googleapis.com/kubernetes-discharge/discharge

/v1.0.6/container/linux/amd64/kubectl

We would now be able to utilize kubectl to see our new group:

$ ./kubectl - kubeconfig=kubeconfig get nodes

We should see a solitary node recorded with the EC2 interior DNS as the name. Note kubeconfig, this reveals to Kubernetes the way to utilize the setup file for the group that was simply created. This is likewise helpful on the off chance that we need to deal with various bunches from a similar machine.

Tectonic

Running Kubernetes on CoreOS is an extraordinary beginning, however you may find that you need a more elevated level of help. Enter Tectonic, the CoreOS venture offering for running Kubernetes with CoreOS. Tectonic uses a significant number of the segments we previously talked about. CoreOS is the OS and both Docker and rkt runtimes are upheld. Likewise, Kubernetes, etcd, and wool are bundled together to give a full heap of group coordination. We talked about wool quickly in Chapter 3, Networking, Load Balancers, and Ingress. It is an overlay arrange that uses a model like the local Kubernetes model, and it utilizes etcd as a backend.

Offering a help bundle like Red Hat, CoreOS likewise gives 24x7 help to the open-source software that Tectonic is based on. Tectonic additionally gives ordinary group refreshes and a pleasant dashboard with sees for every one of the segments of Kubernetes. CoreUpdate enables clients to have more control of the programmed updates. Likewise, it ships with modules for observing, SSO, and other security highlights.

You can discover more data and the most recent guidelines to introduce here:

https://coreos.com/tectonic/docs/most recent/introduce/aws/index.html.

Tectonic is presently commonly accessible and the dashboard as of now has some pleasant highlights.

Another pleasant element is the Events page. Here, we can watch the occasions live, respite, and channel dependent on occasion seriousness and asset type:

A helpful component to peruse anyplace in the dashboard system is the Namespace: sifting alternative. Just snap on the dropdown by the word Namespace: at the highest point of any page that shows assets, and we can channel our perspectives by namespace. This can be useful on the off chance that we need to sift through the Kubernetes system cases or take a gander at a specific assortment of assets:

Summary

In this part, we took a gander at the developing standards bodies in the compartment network and how they are molding the innovation for the better with open particulars. We additionally investigated CoreOS, a key player in both the holder and the Kubernetes people group. We investigated the innovation they are creating to upgrade and praise holder coordination and saw direct how to utilize some of it with Kubernetes. At last, we took a gander at the bolstered venture offering of Tectonic and a portion of the highlights that are accessible at this point.

In the following part, which is the last one, we will investigate the more extensive Kubernetes ecosystem and the apparatuses accessible to move your group from advancement and testing into out and out creation.

Towards Production Ready

In this part, we'll see contemplations to move to creation. We will likewise show some supportive devices and outsider undertakings accessible in the Kubernetes people group everywhere and where you can go to get more help.

This part will talk about the accompanying subjects:

Creation attributes

The Kubernetes ecosystem

Where to find support?

Prepared for creation

We strolled through various run of the mill activities utilizing Kubernetes. As we saw, K8s offers an assortment of highlights and reflections that facilitate the weight of everyday administration for compartment arrangements.

There are numerous attributes that characterize a creation prepared system for holders.

We perceived how the center ideas and deliberations of Kubernetes address a couple of these worries. The administration reflection has worked in administration disclosure and wellbeing checking at both the administration and application level. We additionally get consistent application updates and adaptability from the replication controller and arrangement develops. All the center reflections of administrations, replication controllers, copy sets, and cases work with a center planning and proclivity rulesets and give us simple help and application structure.

There is worked in help for an assortment of tireless stockpiling alternatives, and the systems administration model gives sensible system tasks choices to work with other outsider suppliers. Likewise, we investigated CI/CD incorporation with a portion of the prominent instruments in the commercial center.

Besides, we have worked in system occasions following, and with the significant cloud suppliers, an out-of-the-container arrangement for observing and logging. We additionally perceived how this can be stretched out to outsider suppliers, for example, StackDriver and Sysdig. These administrations likewise address in general node wellbeing and proactive pattern deviation cautions.

The center develops likewise assist us with addressing high accessibility in our application and administration layers. The scheduler can be utilized with autoscaling systems to give this at a node level. At that point there is support for making the Kubernetes ace itself profoundly accessible. In Chapter 9,

Cluster Federation, we investigated the new organization capacities that which guarantee a multi-cloud and multi-datacenter model for what's to come.

We at long last investigated another type of working systems that give us a thin base to expand on and secure update instruments for fixing and updates. The thin base, together with planning, can assist us with effective asset use. Also, we saw some solidified concerns and investigated the picture trust and check devices accessible. Security is a wide theme and abilities network exist for this point alone.

Prepared, set, go

While there are still a few holes, an assortment of the rest of the security and activity concerns are effectively being tended to by outsider organizations, as we will find in the accompanying segment. Going ahead, the Kubernetes venture will proceed to advance, and the network of tasks and accomplices around K8s and Docker will likewise develop. The people group is shutting the rest of the holes at a remarkable pace.

Outsider organizations

Since the Kubernetes task's underlying discharge, there has been a developing ecosystem of accomplices. We took a gander at CoreOS, Sysdig, and numerous others in the past sections, yet there are an assortment of undertakings and organizations in this space. We will feature a not many that might be helpful as you move towards generation. This is in no way, shape or form a thorough rundown and it is just intended to give some intriguing beginning stages.

Private libraries

Much of the time, associations won't have any desire to put their applications and/or protected innovation in open repositories. For those cases, a private vault arrangement is useful in safely incorporating organizations start to finish.

Google Cloud offers the Google Container

Vault at https://cloud.google.com/compartment library/.

Docker has its very own Trusted Registry

offering at https://www.docker.com/docker-trusted-library.

Quay.io additionally gives secure private libraries, powerlessness examining, and originates from the CoreOS group at https://quay.io/.

Google Container Engine

Google was the primary creator of the first Kubernetes venture and is as yet a significant giver. In spite of the fact that this book has for the most part centered around running Kubernetes all alone, Google is additionally offering a completely overseen compartment administration through the Google Cloud Platform.

Discover more data on the Google Container Engine (GKE) site at https://cloud.google.com/compartment motor/.

Kubernetes will be introduced on GCE and will be overseen by Google engineers. They additionally furnish private libraries and incorporation with your current private systems.

Create your first GKE group

From the GCP support, in Compute, click on Container Engine, and then on Container Clusters.

On the off chance that this is your first time making a bunch, you'll have a data confine the center of the page. Snap on the Create a compartment bunch button. Pick a name for your bunch and the zone. You'll likewise have the option to pick the machine type (occasion size) for your nodes and what number of nodes (group size) you need in your bunch. You'll additionally observe a decision for node picture, which gives you a chance to pick the base OS and machine picture for the nodes themselves. The ace is overseen and refreshed by the Google group themselves. Leave Stackdriver Logging and

Stackdriver Monitoring checked. Snap on Create, and in almost no time, you'll have another bunch prepared for use.

You'll require kubectl that is incorporated with the Google SDK to start utilizing your GKE group. Allude to Chapter 1, Introduction to Kubernetes, for subtleties on introducing the SDK. When we have the SDK, we can arrange kubectl and the SDK for our bunch utilizing the means laid out at https://cloud.google.com/holder motor/docs/before-you-begin# install_kubectl.

Sky blue Container Service

Another cloud-oversaw offering is Microsoft's Azure Container Service (ACS). ACS is extremely decent in light of the fact that it enables you to look over industry standard apparatuses, for example, Docker Swarm, Kubernetes, and Mesos. It at that point creates an oversaw group for you, yet utilizes one of these apparatus sets as the establishment. The favorable position is that you can in any case utilize the device's local API and the executives devices, yet leave the administration of the cloud foundation to Azure.

Discover increasingly about ACS at https://azure.microsoft.com/en-us/ administrations/holder administration/.

ClusterHQ

ClusterHQ gives an answer for bringing stateful information into your containerized applications. They give Flocker, an instrument for overseeing relentless stockpiling volumes with compartments, and FlockerHub which gives a capacity vault to your information volumes.

It would be ideal if you allude to the ClusterHQ site for more data at https://clusterhq.com/.

Portworx

Portworx is another player in the extra room. It gives answers for carrying industriousness stockpiling to your compartments. Moreover, it has highlights for snapshotting, encryption, and even multi-cloud replication.

If you don't mind allude to the portworx site for more data at https://portworx.com/.

Shippable

Shippable is a constant joining, persistent sending, and discharge computerization stage that has worked in help for an assortment of current compartment conditions. The item touts supporting any language with a uniform help for bundling and test.

If it's not too much trouble allude to the Shippable site for more data at https://app.shippable.com/.

Twistlock

Twistlock.io is a powerlessness and solidifying apparatus customized for compartments. It gives the capacity to implement strategies, solidifies as indicated by CIS standards, and sweeps images in any famous library for vulnerabilities. It likewise furnishes check joining with famous CI/CD devices and RBAC answers for some, organization apparatuses, for example, Kubernetes.

If you don't mind allude to the Twistlock site for more data at https://www.twistlock.io/.

AquaSec

AquaSec is another security device giving an assortment of highlights. Picture checking with famous libraries, arrangement requirement, client get to control, and compartment solidifying are altogether secured. Also, AquaSec makes them intrigue usefulness in arrange division.

Kindly allude to the Aqua's site for more data at https://www.aquasec.com/.

Mesosphere (Kubernetes on Mesos)

Mesosphere itself is building a monetarily bolstered item (DCOS) around the open-source Apache Mesos venture. Apache Mesos is a group the board system that offers planning and asset sharing somewhat like Kubernetes itself, yet at an a lot more significant level. The open-source venture is utilized by a few surely understood organizations, for example, Twitter and AirBnB.

Get more data on the Mesos OS venture and the Mesosphere offerings at these locales:

http://mesos.apache.org/

https://mesosphere.com/

Mesos by its tendency is particular and permits the utilization of different systems for an assortment of stages. A Kubernetes structure is presently accessible, so we can exploit the group overseeing in Mesos while as yet keeping up the helpful application-level reflections in K8s. Allude to the accompanying connection:

https://github.com/kubernetes-hatchery/kube-mesos-system

Deis

The Deis venture gives an open-source Platform as a Service (PaaS) arrangement dependent on and around Kubernetes. This enables organizations to send their very own PaaS on-premise or on the general population cloud. Deis gives apparatuses to application organization and arrangement, bundle the board (at the unit level), and administration handling.

You can allude to the accompanying site for more data on Deis:

https://deis.com/.

OpenShift

Another PaaS arrangement is OpenShift from Red Hat. The OpenShift stage utilizes the Red Hat Atomic stage as a safe and thin OS for running holders. In adaptation 3, Kubernetes has been included as the arrangement layer for all holder tasks on your PaaS. This is an extraordinary blend to oversee PaaS establishments at an enormous scale.

More data on OpenShift can be found at

https://enterprise.openshift.com/.

Where to find out additional?

The Kubernetes venture is an open-source exertion, so there is an expansive network of benefactors and aficionados. One extraordinary asset so as to discover more help is the Kubernetes Slack channel:

http://slack.kubernetes.io/

There is additionally a Kubernetes bunch on Google gatherings. You can go along with it at

https://groups.google.com/gathering/#!forum/kubernetes-clients.

Summary

We left a couple of breadcrumbs to control you on your proceeded with venture with Kubernetes. You ought to have a strong arrangement of generation attributes to kick you off. There is a wide network in both the Docker and Kubernetes world. There are likewise a couple of extra assets that we gave in the event that you need an amicable face en route.

At this point, we have seen the full range of holder activities with Kubernetes. You ought to be increasingly positive about how Kubernetes can streamline the administration of your holder arrangements and how you can plan to move compartments off the designer workstations onto creation servers. Presently get out there and start transporting your compartments!

Handling the kubernetes Package manager

In this part, we are going to investigate Helm, the Kubernetes bundle chief. Each fruitful and non-minor stage must have a decent bundling system.

Helm was created by Deis (procured by Microsoft 04/2017) and later added to the Kubernetes venture legitimately. We will begin by understanding the inspiration for Helm, its engineering, and its segments. At that point, we'll get hands-on and perceive how to utilize Helm and its graphs inside Kubernetes. That incorporates discovering, introducing, modifying, erasing, and overseeing graphs. To wrap things up, we'll spread how to create your very own graphs and handle forming, conditions, and templating.

The themes we will cover are as per the following:

- Understanding Helm

- Using Helm

- Creating your very own diagrams

Understanding Helm

Kubernetes gives numerous approaches to compose and coordinate your compartments at runtime, however it comes up short on a more elevated level association of collection sets of images together. This is the place Helm comes in. In this segment, we'll go over the inspiration for Helm, its design and parts, and talk about what has changed in the progress from Helm Classic to Helm.

The inspiration for Helm

Helm offers help for a few significant use cases:

•Managing unpredictability

•Easy redesigns

•Simple sharing

•Safe rollbacks

Outlines can depict even the most unpredictable applications, give repeatable application establishment, and fill in as a solitary purpose of power. Set up overhauls and custom snares take into consideration simple updates. It's easy to share graphs that can be formed and facilitated on open or private servers. At the point when you have to rollback late redesigns, Helm gives a solitary command to rollback a strong arrangement of changes to your foundation.

The Helm design

Helm is intended to play out the accompanying:

•Create new outlines without any preparation

•Package outlines into diagram file (tgz) files

•Interact with outline repositories where diagrams are put away

•Install and uninstall outlines into a current Kubernetes bunch

•Manage the discharge cycle of outlines that have been introduced with Helm utilizes a customer server design to accomplish these objectives

Helm segments

Helm has a server segment that sudden spikes in demand for your Kubernetes bunch and a customer part that you run on a neighborhood machine.

The Tiller server

The server is liable for overseeing discharges. It collaborates with the Helm customers just as the Kubernetes API server. Its fundamental capacities are as per the following:

- Listening for approaching solicitations from the Helm customer

- Combining an outline and arrangement to fabricate a discharge

- Installing outlines into Kubernetes

- Tracking the ensuing discharge

- Upgrading and uninstalling outlines by collaborating with Kubernetes

The Helm customer

You introduce the Helm customer on your machine. It is answerable for the accompanying:

- Local outline advancement

- Managing repositories

- Interacting with the Tiller server

- Sending outlines to be introduced

- Asking for data about discharges

- Requesting redesigns or uninstallation of existing discharges

Helm versus. Helm-exemplary

Helm was initially created by Deis until adaptation 0.70. From that point forward, the first Helm has been branded Helm-great. The main motivation to utilize Helm-exemplary is in the event that you as of now have existing diagrams and you're

not prepared to update. Helm great is accessible here:

https://github.com/helm/helm-classic.git.

Utilizing Helm

Helm is a rich bundle the executives system that gives you a chance to play out all the fundamental strides to deal with the applications introduced on your group. How about we focus in and get moving.

Introducing Helm

Introducing Helm includes introducing the customer and the server. Helm is actualized in Go, and a similar double executable can fill in as either customer or server.

Introducing the Helm customer

You should have Kubectl arranged appropriately to converse with your Kubernetes group on the grounds that the Helm customer utilizes the Kubectl arrangement to converse with the Helm server (Tiller)

Helm gives parallel discharges to all stages here: https://github.com/ kubernetes/helm/discharges/most recent.

For Windows, it is your solitary choice.

For Mac OSX and Linux, you can introduce the customer from a content:

$ twist https://raw.githubusercontent.com/kubernetes/helm/ace/contents/ get > get_helm.sh

$ chmod 700 get_helm.sh

$ ./get_helm.sh

On Mac OSX, you can likewise utilize Homebrew:

mix introduce kubernetes-helm

Introducing the Tiller server

Tiller ordinarily runs inside your group. For improvement, it is now and again simpler to run Tiller locally.

Introducing Tiller in-bunch

The most effortless approach to introduce Tiller is from a machine where the Helm customer is introduced. Run the accompanying command: helm init.

This will instate both the customer just as the Tiller server on the remote Kubernetes bunch. At the point when the establishment is done, you will have a running Tiller unit in the kube-system namespace of your group:

$ kubectl get po - namespace=kube-system - l name=tiller

NAMEREADYSTATUSRESTARTSAGE

tiller-convey 3210613906-2j5sh1/1Running01m

You can likewise run helm variant to look at both the customer's and the server's form:

$ helm form

Customer: &version.Version{SemVer:"v2.2.3",
GitCommit:"1402a4d6ec9fb349e17b   912e32fe259ca21181e3",
GitTreeState:"clean"}

Server: &version.Version{SemVer:"v2.2.3",
GitCommit:"1402a4d6ec9fb349e17b   912e32fe259ca21181e3",
GitTreeState:"clean"}

Introducing Tiller locally

In the event that you need to run Tiller locally, you have to assemble it first. This is bolstered on Linux

and Mac OSX:

$ disc $GOPATH

$ mkdir - p src/k8s.io

$ disc src/k8s.io

$ git clone https://github.com/kubernetes/helm.git

$ disc helm

$ make bootstrap construct

The bootstrap target will endeavor to introduce conditions, remake the merchant/tree, and approve design.

The fabricate target will arrange Helm and spot it in canister/helm. Tiller is additionally arranged and is set in canister/tiller.

Presently you can simply run container/tiller. Tiller will interface with the Kubernetes bunch by means of your Kubectl setup.

You have to advise the Helm customer to associate with the neighborhood Tiller server. You can do it by setting a situation variable:

$ send out HELM_HOST=localhost:44134

Or then again you can pass it as a command-line contention, - have localhost:44134.

Discovering diagrams

So as to introduce valuable applications and software with Helm, you have to discover their graphs first. This is the place the helm search command comes in. Helm, as a matter of course, look through the official Kubernetes diagram store, which is called stable:

$ helm search

NAMEVERSION DESCRIPTION

stable/chaoskube0.5.0Chaoskube intermittently executes random cases in you...

stable/cockroachdb0.2.2CockroachDB is an adaptable, survivable, unequivocally...

stable/dokuwiki0.1.3DokuWiki is a standards-agreeable, easy to us...

stable/jenkins0.3.1Open source constant joining server. It s...

stable/kapacitor motor. It ca...0.2.2InfluxDB's local information handling

stable/kube-lego declarations from Let's

...0.1.8Automatically demands

stable/kube-operations see read-just system ...0.2.0Kubernetes Operational View -

stable/kube2iam dependent on annota...0.2.1Provide IAM certifications to cases

The official archive has a rich library of outlines that speak to all cutting edge open source databases, checking systems, Kubernetes-explicit aides, and a huge number of different offerings, for example, a Minecraft server. You can scan for explicit outlines. For instance, how about we scan for graphs that contain kube in their name or depiction:

$ helm search kube

NAMEVERSION DESCRIPTION

stable/chaoskube0.5.0Chaoskube intermittently slaughters random units in you...

stable/kube-lego0.1.8Automatically demands testaments from Let's ...

stable/kube-operations view0.2.0Kubernetes Operational View - read-just system ...

stable/kube2iam0.2.1Provide IAM accreditations to units dependent on annota...

stable/sumokube0.1.1Sumologic Log Collector

stable/etcd-operator0.2.0CoreOS etcd-administrator Helm diagram for Kubernetes

stable/nginx-lego0.2.1Chart for nginx-entrance controller and kube-lego

stable/openvpn1.0.1A Helm diagram to introduce an openvpn server insid...

stable/spartakus1.1.1Collect data about Kubernetes bunches t...

stable/traefik1.1.2-h A Traefik based Kubernetes entrance controller w...

How about we attempt another inquiry:

$ helm search mysql

NAMEVERSION DESCRIPTION

stable/mysql0.2.5Fast, solid, adaptable, and simple to utilize open-

...

stable/mariadb0.5.14Fast, solid, adaptable, and simple to utilize open-

...

What was the deal? For what reason does mariadb appear in the outcomes? The explanation is that mariadb (which is a fork of MySQL) makes reference to MySQL in its portrayal, despite the fact that you can't see it in the truncated yield. To get the full depiction, utilize the helm examine command:

$ helm assess stable/mariadb

portrayal: Fast, solid, versatile, and simple to utilize open-source social database

system. MariaDB Server is planned for crucial, overwhelming burden generation systems just as for installing into mass-conveyed software. motor: gotpl

home: https://mariadb.org

symbol: https://bitnami.com/resources/stacks/mariadb/img/ mariadb-stack-220x234.png

watchwords:

- mariadb

- mysql

- database

- sql maintainers:

- email: containers@bitnami.com name: Bitnami

name: mariadb sources:

- https://github.com/bitnami/bitnami-docker-mariadb rendition: 0.5.14

Introducing bundles

Alright. You've discovered the bundle you had always wanted. Presently, you most likely need to introduce it on your Kubernetes group. At the point when you introduce a bundle, Helm creates a discharge

that you can use to monitor the establishment progress. We should introduce MariaDB utilizing the helm introduce command. How about we go over the yield in detail. The initial segment of the yield records the name of the discharge - alert-panda for this situation (you can pick your very own with the - name banner), the namespace, and the arrangement status:

$ helm introduce stable/mariadb NAME:alert-panda

LAST DEPLOYED: Sat Apr1 18:39:47 2017

NAMESPACE: default STATUS: DEPLOYED

The second piece of the yield records every one of the assets created by this outline. Note that the asset names are altogether gotten from the discharge name.

Assets:

==> v1/PersistentVolumeClaim

NAMESTATUSVOLUMECAPACITYACCESSMODESAGE

alert-panda-mariadbPending1s

==> v1/Service

NAME

Bunch IP

Outer IP

PORT(S)AGE

alert-panda-mariadb10.3.245.245<none>3306/TCP1s

==> augmentations/v1beta1/Deployment

NAMEDESIREDCURRENTUP-TO-DATEAVAILABLEAGE

alert-panda-mariadb11101s

==> v1/Secret NAME

TYPE

Information

AGE

alert-panda-mariadbOpaque21s

==> v1/ConfigMap

NAMEDATAAGE

alert-panda-mariadb11s

The last part is takes note of that give straightforward directions on the most proficient method to utilize

MariaDB in the substance of your Kubernetes bunch. NOTES:

MariaDB can be gotten to by means of port 3306 on the accompanying DNS name from inside your bunch:

alert-panda-mariadb.default.svc.cluster.local

To associate with your database:

1.Run a case that you can use as a customer:

kubectl run alert-panda-mariadb-customer - rm - tty - I - picture bitnami/ mariadb - command - slam

2.Connect utilizing the mysql cli, at that point give your secret phrase:

$ mysql - h alert-panda-mariadb

Checking establishment status

Helm doesn't trust that the establishment will finish since it might take some time. The helm status command shows the most recent data on a discharge in a similar configuration as the yield of the underlying helm introduce command. In the yield of the introduce command you can see that the tireless volume guarantee had a pending status. We should look at it now:

$ helm status alert-panda | grep Persist - A 3

==> v1/PersistentVolumeClaim

NAMESTATUS VOLUMECAPACITY ACCESSMODESAGE

alert-panda-mariadbBoundpvc-41... 0156 8GiRWO10m

Yippee! It is bound now, and there is a volume joined with 8 GB limit.

We should attempt to interface and check mariadb is in fact available. We should alter the recommended commands a smidgen from the notes to interface. Rather than running slam and then running mysql, we can legitimately run the mysql command on the compartment:

$ kubectl run alert-panda-mariadb-customer - rm - tty - I - picture bitnami/ mariadb - command - mysql - h al

ert-panda-mariadb

On the off chance that you don't see a command brief, take a stab at squeezing enter.

MariaDB [(none)]> show databases;

| Database|

| information_schema |

| mysql|

| performance_schema |

3 lines in set (0.00 sec)

Modifying a graph

Frequently as a client, you need to redo or design the graphs you introduce. Helm completely bolsters customization by means of config files. To find out about conceivable customizations you can utilize the helm examine command once more, yet this time center around the qualities.

Here is a halfway yield:

$ helm investigate values stable/mariadb ## Bitnami MariaDB picture adaptation

ref: https://hub.docker.com/r/bitnami/mariadb/labels/##

Default: none

picture: bitnami/mariadb:10.1.22-r1

Specify an imagePullPolicy (Required)

It's prescribed to change this to 'Consistently' if the picture tag is 'most recent'

ref: http://kubernetes.io/docs/client direct/images/#updating-images imagePullPolicy: IfNotPresent

Specify secret phrase for root client

##ref: https://github.com/bitnami/bitnami-docker-mariadb/mass/ace/ README.md#setting-the-root-secret phrase on-first-run

##

mariadbRootPassword:

Create a database client

##ref: https://github.com/bitnami/bitnami-docker-mariadb/mass/ace/ README.md#creating-a-database-client on-first-run

##

mariadbUser:

mariadbPassword:

Create a database

##ref: https://github.com/bitnami/bitnami-docker-mariadb/mass/ace/ README.md#creating-a-database-on-first-run

##

mariadbDatabase:

For instance, on the off chance that you need to set a root secret key and create a database when introducing mariadb, you can create the accompanying YAML file and spare it as mariadb-config.yaml:

mariadbRootPassword: supersecret mariadbDatabase: awesome_stuff

At that point, run helm and pass it the yaml file: helm introduce - f config.yaml stable/mariadb

You can likewise set individual qualities on the command line with - set. In the event that both - f and - set attempt to set similar qualities, at that point - set comes first. For instance, for this situation the root secret key will be evenbettersecret:

Helm introduce - f config.yaml - set mariadbRootPassword=evenbettersecret stable/mariadb

You can indicate numerous qualities utilizing comma-isolated records: - set a=1,b=2.

Extra establishment choices

The helm introduce command can introduce from a few sources:

- A diagram storehouse (as we've seen)

- A neighborhood graph document (helm introduce foo-0.1.1.tgz)

- An unloaded diagram catalog (helm introduce way/to/foo)

- A full URL (helm introduce https://example.com/diagrams/foo-1.2.3.tgz)

Updating and moving back a discharge

You might need to update a bundle you introduced to the best in class adaptation. Helm give the redesign command, which works wisely and just updates things that have changed. For instance, how about we check the present estimations of our mariadb establishment:

$ helm get values alert-panda mariadbDatabase: awesome_stuff mariadbRootPassword: evenbettersecret

Presently, we should run, overhaul, and change the name of the database:

$ helm overhaul alert-panda - set mariadbDatabase=awesome_sauce stable/ mariadb

$ helm get values alert-panda mariadbDatabase: awesome_sauce

Note that we've lost our root secret phrase. All the current qualities are supplanted when you overhaul. Alright, allow's move to back. The helm history command gives all of us the accessible updates we can move back to:

$ helm history alert-panda

REVISION	STATUS	CHART
1	SUPERSEDED	mariadb-0.5.14
2	SUPERSEDED	mariadb-0.5.14
3	SUPERSEDED	mariadb-0.5.14
4	DEPLOYED	mariadb-0.5.14

Let's roll back to revision 3:

$ helm rollback alert-panda 3

Rollback was a success! Happy Helming!

$ helm history alert-panda

REVISION	**STATUS**	**CHART**
1	SUPERSEDED	mariadb-0.5.14
2	SUPERSEDED	mariadb-0.5.14
3	SUPERSEDED	mariadb-0.5.14
4	SUPERSEDED	mariadb-0.5.14
5	DEPLOYED	mariadb-0.5.14

Let's verify our changes were rolled back:

$ helm get values alert-panda mariadbDatabase: awesome_stuff mariadbRootPassword: evenbettersecret

Summary

In this section, we investigated Helm, the Kubernetes bundle chief. Helm enables Kubernetes to oversee muddled software made out of numerous Kubernetes assets with between conditions. It fills a similar need as an OS bundle administrator. It sorts out bundles and gives you a chance to look through diagrams, introduce and redesign graphs, and offer outlines with teammates. You can build up your outlines and store them in repositories.

Now, you ought to understand the significant job that Helm serves in the Kubernetes ecosystem and network. You ought to have the option to utilize it beneficially and even create and share your own outlines.

Don't miss out!

Visit the website below and you can sign up to receive emails whenever Jordan Lioy publishes a new book. There's no charge and no obligation.

https://books2read.com/r/B-A-GYIX-OPQGC

BOOKS 2 READ

Connecting independent readers to independent writers.

Did you love *Kubernetes: Build and Deploy Modern Applications in a Scalable Infrastructure. The Complete Guide to the Most Modern Scalable Software Infrastructure.*? Then you should read *Docker: The Complete Guide to the Most Widely Used Virtualization Technology. Create Containers and Deploy them to Production Safely and Securely.*[1] by Jordan Lioy!

This is the best book to learn Docker from zero.Docker is the virtualization architecture of the future.

With this book you will learn...• The basics - the theory behind Docker• *Extensive coverage of Docker architecture*• Deep dive into core concepts such as images and containers• *How Docker can organize your projects*• Networking, volumes, and security• *Docker Certified Associate (DCA) coverage*

And much, much more, with a lot of examples to help you understand and implement every solution.

---

1. https://books2read.com/u/mvyGpX

2. https://books2read.com/u/mvyGpX

Also by Jordan Lioy

Docker & Kubernetes

Docker: The Complete Guide to the Most Widely Used Virtualization Technology. Create Containers and Deploy them to Production Safely and Securely.
Kubernetes: Build and Deploy Modern Applications in a Scalable Infrastructure. The Complete Guide to the Most Modern Scalable Software Infrastructure.

Standalone

Software Containers: The Complete Guide to Virtualization Technology. Create, Use and Deploy Scalable Software with Docker and Kubernetes. Includes Docker and Kubernetes.